Religion and Human Fulfilment

Religion and Human Fulfilment

Keith Ward

scm press

British Library Cataloguing in Publication data

A catalogue record for this book is available
from the British Library

978 0 334 04163 4

First published in 2008 by SCM Press
13–17 Long Lane,
London EC1A 9PN

www.scm-canterburypress.co.uk

SCM Press is a division of
SCM-Canterbury Press Ltd

Typeset by Regent Typesetting, London
Printed in the UK by CPI William Clowes Beccles NR34 7TL

Contents

This book is based on the John Albert Hall lectures, given at the University of Victoria, Canada, and the Gresham College lectures given in London in 2006.

Prologue

Soon after I had delivered the lectures on which this book is based,[1] a flurry of popular books appeared attacking the whole idea of religion as irrational and immoral. Richard Dawkins' *The God Delusion*, Daniel Dennett's *Breaking the Spell*, Christopher Hitchen's *God is Not Great* and Sam Harris's *Letter to a Christian Nation* all set a new tone of virulent aggression against the evils of religion.

Since my lectures rather assumed that the major world faiths at least attempt to promote human fulfilment, and to be forces for good in the world, the appearance of these books was quite a shock. Did I have too rosy and cosy a view of religion? Had I been blind to its intrinsic evils? Was I quite wrong, and had I simply overlooked the fact that religion in fact is opposed to everything that might promote human flourishing?

At the very least I had underestimated the hatred that religion inspires in some very intelligent and voluble people. I do feel the need to give some account of how this can be so. Of course there are some very obvious features of the modern world that might inspire dislike and antipathy. Seeing people praying to God for the destruction of innocent people, and thanking God for what most of us would call terrorist acts, any person of reasonable good will would feel a sense of moral revulsion. Not all religion is good religion, and there is a very easy and clear rule for when a religion is bad. Whenever religion increases hatred, intolerance and oppression, it is

---

1 John Albert Hall Lecture Series, University of Victoria, Canada, October 2006, and lectures given at Gresham College, London, 2006.

bad religion. Whenever religion increases ignorance, unreasoned belief and prejudice, it is bad religion.

There is plenty of bad religion about. But it is pretty obvious that if religion gets into the hands of bad people, then it will be bad. The capacity of human minds to twist even the most benign scriptural texts into something morally corrupt is huge. In the case of Christianity, for instance, the good news that God entered into the human world to redeem humans from evil can be, and has been, turned into the not so good news that God entered the world so that most people would be damned for ever, when they refused to recognize him.

Any religion that calls for the killing of unbelievers, or that curtails the freedom of critical thought, or that stops people thinking for themselves, is bad. All ministers of religion know that some people are psychologically damaged by religion, or by what they think or have been told is religion. So the religion-haters have a point. There is a lot of evil about in the world, and some forms of religion can make it worse.

However, the very fact that we can say what bad religion is shows that it is at least logically possible to have good religion as well as bad. Good religion will be the opposite of bad religion. It will be religion that increases love, understanding, tolerance, critical thought and care for the oppressed and those who suffer.

So good religion is possible. But is there any? To answer that question you have to have some idea of what religion is. At this point the recent opponents of religion ignore the work of most sociologists and anthropologists of religion, like Emile Durkheim and Edward Evans-Pritchard, and just make up their own theories from scratch.

Daniel Dennett, appealing to the Darwinian method that he seems to think explains virtually everything, proceeds to give a Darwinian account of the origins of religion. Some religious acts or beliefs may be explained as features which preferentially enhanced the replication and survival of human groups in the far past. For instance, if a ritual enhances feelings of group solidarity and loyalty, that group may be better at exterminating its rivals. This seems a reasonable, if incomplete, explanation. But there is a major problem. As Evans-Pritchard points out in his classic book, *Theories of Primitive Religion*[2] we have virtually no reliable information about the origins of religion. Written records go back to the fourth millennium BCE at best, and before that we have to guess what the graves and remains of early human cultures signified to people of that time. Dennett's method is to say, 'If I had been a cave-man, I would have been very stupid and ignorant; so I would probably have had lots of false theories about thunderstorms and earthquakes being caused by invisible gods. So that is probably what early religion was.' This inevitably looks more like a bit of speculative philosophy than any sort of hard science. Thus we are told that early humans took their religious beliefs literally, which there is no possible way of knowing. And we are told that the earliest form of religious belief was animism – the natural if child-like delusion that everything in the world has intentions and feelings. This developed into theism, basically because one all-powerful God can give a better pay-off than many conflicting spirits. Well, maybe so. But most anthropologists consider that regarding early religion as a failed attempt at science is quite the wrong approach. The nature of pre-literate religion is almost completely hidden to us, but studies of non-literate religion suggest many other forms of possible explanation.

Among them is the view that some humans believe that they apprehend the presence of a transcendent reality – transcendent in being other and more than any empirical object in space-time, and in having an objective moral value that is felt to inspire or command. Anthropologists usually now try to record such beliefs, without asking whether there is any transcendent reality in fact.

It seems to me that one should at least keep an open mind on the issue. It also seems quite possible that there is such a transcendent

---

2 E. E. Evans-Pritchard, *Theories of Primitive Religion*, Oxford: Clarendon Press, 1965.

object of supreme value, though humans will interpret experience of it in ways influenced by their language, history and culture. Perhaps the many gods and spirits of some non-literate religions record different aspects under which such a reality appears. That seems a reasonable speculation to me.

Naturally, this is as speculative as Dennett's account, though no more so. The point is that a present-day believer in God will not be disposed to think that early religion is a primitive form of science. They may rather think that it is a primitive form of interpreting a perception of a transcendent being, or beings, of great moral value. In saying this is primitive, we would be adopting an evolutionary view of religion, as of everything else human. We might think this would appeal to Dawkins and Dennett, because it is a view that owes much to Darwin's method (though the evolutionary view owes as much to Hegel in this case). But they both seem to commit the elementary mistake of thinking that the earliest, most primitive, forms of religion are its genuine and essential forms.

If anyone tried to say that the only genuine science is Aristotelian, or even pre-Aristotelian science, that would be laughable – or, as Dawkins likes to say, barking mad. The same is true of morality. Dawkins points out that moral views have changed considerably even in the last century. So we should not dream of taking Bronze Age moral principles as our final guides today.

For some unfathomable reason, they do not allow the same principles to apply to religion. If it was ever Bronze Age, it always has to remain Bronze Age. It is supremely ironic that the main popular proponents of evolution deny that there can be change or evolution in religion. Yet the Bible gives one of the best records we have of change and development in religious beliefs over many centuries.

From early belief in one tribal god among others to the eighth-century BCE prophetic insight that there is only one God who wills justice for the whole earth, the Bible records a huge development of thought about God. That development continues throughout history, and it seems likely that no developed concept of God held by theologians today is identical to concepts held by people three thousand years ago. There has been change, rationally and morally, and that change has affected, and has in turn been influenced by, religious beliefs. Change is not always for the better, and it is a very sad fact that some recent changes in religion have decidedly been for the worse. The resurgence of fundamentalism is one of these changes for the worse. Fundamentalism arises because sacred texts have been made available in translation to all, and the freedom of critical enquiry that the Enlightenment made possible has encouraged personal and idiosyncratic interpretations of these texts that reject all traditional religious scholarship.

Fundamentalism, in other words, is a product of modernity, of freedom of information and interpretation. These things in themselves are great values. But they have resulted in the spread of weird and uninstructed beliefs about religion – beliefs that Dennett and Dawkins strangely seem to share. The chief of these is that religious texts provide direct and infallible information about the creation of the universe and about the moral principles we should follow, and – in the most virulent forms of fundamentalism – that they encourage us to eliminate all who disagree with us.

Dennett and Dawkins have been so indoctrinated with this very modern and revisionist idea of religious belief that they seem honestly to think this is what religion really is. Dawkins even claims that he does not know what 'theology' could be – though he is surrounded by some of the world's most distinguished theologians. That is a typical fundamentalist refusal to accept that change (produced by reflective thought) and reinterpretation (produced by greater knowledge of cosmic and human nature) are important parts of religious belief. That is an important part of what theologians do – they reformulate ancient beliefs to take account of new knowledge and insights. Fundamentalists and Dawkins alike reject theology. In doing so, they reject the quest for understanding and truth that has marked universities since their foundation.

In fact this is a point at which I get mad at Dawkins, a man whose writings on science I much admire. The aim of a university education is to produce greater understanding and a more reasoned approach to the great questions of the meaning, value and purposes (if any) of human life, as they are treated in science, art, history, philosophy, and religion. A first requirement for doing this is to encourage an initial empathetic understanding of views other than one's own. Yes, this is even true of Hitler's National Socialism or Lenin's version of communism. If you cannot state a view in a way a believer could recognize as accurate, then you cannot be said to have understood it.

But it is important, second, to have a knowledge in depth of alternative views. This helps to give a sense of the precariousness of all human thought, and of the inevitable diversity of human interpretations of experience.

Third, having an awareness of the strong and weak points of your own position, you should seek to come to a balanced judgement, realizing that equally intelligent people will not all agree, but that sometimes you have to reject some views (like National Socialism) outright, even though you have managed initially to state them empathetically.

These three rules for rational understanding are basic and vital. Regrettably, Dawkins breaks all of them in his consideration of religion. Thereby he undermines the basic principles of a humane university education. And I do think that is a disgrace for any university professor. However, enough of my anger – which is not about the rejection of religion, but about the way in which a topic of great human and intellectual importance is treated (whether or not you have any religious beliefs). The major point is that the cultivation of a historical sense will free anyone from fundamentalism, and allow it to be seen as a modern aberration which thrives only by rejecting the major traditions of thought in religion. Fundamentalism is bad religion because it encourages ignorance, ignorance about how religions change and develop and decay, as well as, usually, about what the sciences say about the world.

If religions change, they may change for better or worse. Is there, though, something about religion itself that makes it have a tendency to irrationality or immorality? Its modern detractors seem to think there is, but when they attempt to say what it is, their arguments turn into shrill squeaks.

Religion is irrational, Dawkins says, because it applauds 'unquestioning belief', blind faith, and degrading deference to authority. Well, some religious views do, just as some moral views do. But if the heart of religion is belief that there is a transcendent reality of supreme value (some call it 'God'), that hardly seems unquestioning, blind or degrading. Such a belief has been defended by almost every great classical philosopher, from Plato through Descartes, Leibniz, Locke, and Kant to Hegel. It has been defended after intense critical examination, as a rational and plausible basic world-view.[3] Dawkins and company may disagree, but there is something substantive and important to disagree about. It is not a matter of obvious truth versus lamentable delusion. Anyone who claims to value the provisional and incomplete nature of all human knowledge should be ready to acknowledge that.

I agree that we need to discover why people have a tendency to claim certainty where there is none, and to hanker after magic rather than be content with more prosaic facts. These are questions for psychology, and I doubt if it helps to say that 'religion' causes people to do so. All we can say is that some religions, like some moral and political systems, show such human tendencies to be at work. Good religion, being eminently reasonable, will try to curb them. But is good, reasonable belief in a transcendent supreme value being defeated in our contemporary world by irrational beliefs in magic and uncritical assent to authority? Perhaps it is. What, then, should be our response? We could say, with Dawkins, that all religion should be put aside (but that is not going to happen). Or we could argue for a reasoned, critical, approach to religion (this is what all

---

3 I have given what I believe to be a fairly conclusive reply to Dawkins in *Pascal's Fire*, Oxford: Oneworld Publications, 2006.

the Oxford theologians I know do). It surely will not do to say that, since some religion is held irrationally, therefore all religion is in danger of being irrational. After all, Darwinism may be held irrationally. It has been, by Haeckel in Nazi Germany and by those who think it justifies exterminating the genetically weak. The correct response is not to abandon Darwinism, but to counter irrationalism in science as a perversion of what it should be.

The same is true of religion. It may be true that a conscious being of supreme value exists as the creator of this universe. The hypothesis has been and still is rationally defended. It is just embarrassing to be told that all such defences are poor, when they have not even been read or taken seriously by their critics, and when they are as badly parodied as they are by Dawkins in *The God Delusion*.

But the more serious charge against religion is that it tends to make people immoral. It encourages intolerance, violence, and unacceptable 'moral' principles. No one denies that some religious views do this. The question is only whether there is something about religion, as such, that inevitably leads to such tendencies.

Suppose you have a religion that explicitly says, 'You must not be intolerant' and 'You must not resort to violence'. How could such a religion encourage intolerance and violence? Extraordinarily, of course, Christians have a religion that says, 'You must love your neighbour as yourself', and 'Everyone is your neighbour, even people you dislike and oppose'. Yet Christians have killed and burned each other at the stake. It almost passes comprehension, and it really is impossible to explain as following from Christian moral principles.

There must be some other explanation. A general religious explanation is that humans are enslaved to hatred and passion. They will pervert even the highest principles to their selfish ends. So when they get hold of a religion, they will pervert that too. But it is not the religion that is causing the hatred. It is the hatred that is causing the religion to become perverse. That is what is happening in the modern world with Islamic jihadists. They hate the West because of the chaos and destruction that Western forces have, the jihadists believe, caused in the Middle East. Given such burning hatred, religious texts, taken out of context and without reference to centuries of careful scholarly interpretation, can be used to give a 'moral' justification for terrorism. Most Muslims recognize this as a perversion of Islam, even though some might sympathize with the desire for revenge that Jihadists have. Jews and Christians have also had their terrorists. Yet with all of them, but especially strongly with Christianity, terrorism is clearly incompatible with the teaching of mercy and loving-kindness that is professed most explicitly in the Christian Sermon on the Mount, which seems to call for total non-violence.

Once again, we desperately need help in understanding the strands of religious thought that lend themselves to perversion in this way, and in finding ways to counteract such perversions. Religious views usually have strong moral implications, and it is the case that traditional attitudes, as well as modernist fundamentalism, can stand in the way of recognizing some modern advances in understanding human nature that have strong moral relevance.

Religion, like morality and politics, can never be free of argument and disputation. Indeed, argument (or dialectic, as Plato called it) is the life-blood of moral advance. Today on moral questions religions often find themselves caught in a trilemma of conservative traditionalism, which refuses to recognize there have been some moral advances in the world in recent decades; modernist fundamentalism, which insists on a scriptural literalism that simply ignores modern science altogether; and liberal revisionism, which threatens to leave religious faith with no important content to defend. It is the purpose of this book to cut through that trilemma by defending a liberal and critical view of religion that leaves it with a distinctive and life-enhancing view of the world, and with a vitally important moral content.

Dawkins and company may think the task is impossible and not worth spending energy on. The forces of reaction and ignorance are bound to win, in religion, they think. Well, there are religious views that agree, and that add, even more pessimistically, that the forces of reaction and ignorance are bound to win in every area of human life. Science itself, with its self-proclaimed love of truth and understanding, is much more likely than religion to destroy the earth, by devising biological and nuclear weapons of unstoppable destructive power, and by rendering the earth uninhabitable precisely by its ceaseless pursuit of more energy-consuming technologies.

How, then, can the earth be saved? One starting-point is to change the human heart, by nature intolerant, abusive, and over-dogmatic, to become more tolerant, reconciliatory and tentative in its broad-ranging theories. Where can we find the resources to do that? Not, it seems, in every form of religious faith, and not in some peculiarly adversarial forms of popular atheistic writing either.

One resource – I do not say it is the only one – is a sincere belief in an objective transcendent reality of supreme value, of compassion, self-giving love, mercy and forgiveness. In the practice of seeking to apprehend such a supreme value, and to incorporate its nature into your own life, there may be a transformation of the heart to love the good for its own sake alone. That is a religious practice. It is in fact the central religious practice of prayer and meditation in all the major world religions. I fail to see how such a practice could be called either irrational or immoral. But I entirely accept that there are elements in all religions that do encourage irrationality and immorality. I accept that it is vitally important to identify such elements and seek to counter them. The new atheists perform a service in reminding believers of their hypocrisies and self-deceptions. But perhaps they do not see quite so clearly how all human beliefs, religious or not, are prone to irrational and immoral moments.

It does not take more than a few hours research to discover many of them in science. No human activity is free from the tendency to evil. But I suspect that when religion is singled out as a special cause of evil, it is simply being used as a scapegoat. 'That is where the evil comes from,' the atheists say, 'it does not come from us; we are free of all such taints.' What, free of prejudice, stereotypes, over-generalization, stigmatization, and parody? Perhaps not quite.

Overall, then, I do not think I have taken too rosy a view of religion, though I have certainly tried to stress its positive possibilities. But it could all go wrong. The forces of ignorance and credulity could triumph. All I would say is that it does not have to be that way. Perhaps we should do all we can to make sure it is not that way.

Despite all the manifest perversions and dangers of religion in human history, I believe that religion is essentially concerned with finding the best way in which humans can flourish. There are many problems about discovering what this is, and many disagreements about it. But a more careful and nuanced study of religion than the new atheists have given us might find that religion and morality, if they work together, have something important to teach us. But on one point I agree with the new atheists. Religion has to change today, as it has had to change many times in the past. It is in changing, rather than seeking to recover an allegedly unchangeable past that religion might find its essential nature.

How should it change? By an alliance with that strong moral concern for human flourishing that was a major feature of Enlightenment humanism. Humanism is itself under threat from a more combative scientific materialism that regards reverence for human life as speciesist prejudice, and appeals to morality as calls for submission to outdated tribal loyalties.

The sad thing is that, at least in Britain, in the early years of the twentieth century, the dominant forms of religion and philosophy saw the heart of reality in a supreme consciousness of goodness and beauty. They saw the evolutionary story of humankind as one of moving towards fuller awareness of that cosmic consciousness, an awareness that would mediate its goodness and beauty in the temporal world.

What went wrong? How has much philosophy (not all, by any means) become so materialistic and reductionist? How has much religion (thankfully not all) become so literalist and inward-looking? There are many reasons, but one thing is clear: like the First and Second World Wars (totally non-religious but ferociously destructive), the nations of the world turned away from the idealism of faith in objective goodness to the brutal realities of the will to power. If such a self-destructive turn is to be reversed, more humane forms of religion and more idealistic visions of human nature will need to be rediscovered. The hate-filled and prejudice-distorted books of the new atheists are explosions of revulsion against all that religion and morality are when they become instruments of the will to power. All the more important, then, to move into a more positive mode, and find what it is in religion and morality that could give hope for the world. That is what this book attempts to do.

Introduction

Religion, Humanism, and Transcendental Personalism

Religion takes many forms, but one continuing concern of most religions has been a search for human fulfilment, for a way of life that will achieve what is believed to be the true purpose of human existence.

For many people, there is no such true purpose. They believe that human beings have arisen by chance in a universe without purpose, and if humans are to have any purpose in life, they must construct it for themselves. There is no objective goal that they must or should reach. Most major religions, however, posit that there is such an objective goal. It may be liberation from desire and suffering (as in Buddhism, for example), or the knowledge and love of a supremely good personal being (in theistic faiths like Christianity), or a life in harmony with the inherent moral laws of the cosmos (the Tao or Way of Heaven, in different forms of Chinese traditional thought).

The post-Renaissance movement known as 'humanism' generally maintains that there are moral ideals and duties that humans should respect, and that human life is of distinctive worth. In particular, a good life is one that realizes distinctively personal excellences, such as intellectual understanding, creative action, social co-operation and compassion. This is not generally thought by those who call themselves humanists to be an objective purpose for human life. But it is nevertheless a moral ideal, depicting a good life, for all human beings. One main underlying question of this book is whether it is intellectually satisfactory to posit a moral ideal for humans as such

1

without any idea of a moral purpose. We may be devoted to the flourishing of human culture just because we are interested in it. But that is hardly a moral ideal; it is a matter of taste, and 'high culture' may be widely regarded as an elitist option for the rich or leisured. A real moral ideal should be universal, and it is hard to see the basis for making devotion to culture and self-realization a universal obligation if one thinks that each person is morally free to choose for themselves how they should live.

Humanism, as a cultural movement, has at least two main forms. One form treats human life without regard for any supernatural forces, and seeks some sort of sustainable morality for the complex, passionate and often irrational beings that humans are. For this form, personal freedom to act as one wishes, as long as such action does not harm others, is of primary importance. But there is another strand of humanism, for which there is a universal ideal of realizing human intellectual and moral capacities to the fullest practicable extent. In the work of John Stuart Mill these two forms of humanism uneasily coexist.

Mill's view could be put by saying that people should be permitted to be free to do whatever does not directly cause obvious harm to others. But what they really ought to do is pursue the fullest realization of their distinctively personal capacities. Mill is in the end a believer in universal obligations, even though he does not think we should, or can, force people to meet them. This is one classical statement of liberal humanism.

I prefer to call it 'personalism', in order to avoid the charge that humanism is simply a prejudice in favour of the human species. It is a philosophy concerned with the flourishing of personal capacities – capacities of intellect, free and creative action, and responsible relationships – whatever species such personal beings might belong to.

What could justify the assertion that such a moral ideal of personal flourishing is universally binding? Another prominent philosopher of the Enlightenment, Immanuel Kant, argued that it is binding simply because it can be universally willed without contradiction. But he assumed all along that Reason is a practical, active power, so that it is Reason that drives each person to extend their cultural capacities. And at just that point Kant's crucial move is revealed, from regarding God as an objective and external personal being who issues commands that we have to obey unquestioningly, to seeing God as an internal and active principle of Reason progressively realizing itself in human lives, to whose decrees our subjective reason will, if it is freed from the temptations of desire, unhesitatingly assent.

This is what might be called a form of transcendental personalism – seeing in personal self-realization the expression of the true nature and purpose of human, and perhaps of cosmic, existence. This purpose is inherent in human life, not imposed as a set of rules from without. It is an inner purpose, discernible by a study of human nature, not an external set of rules, knowable only by revelation. It is an expression of the drive of cosmic evolution to realize its nature in fully personal forms of manifestation.

Why should persons flourish? Because that is the goal of Reason. It is, for Kant, one of the 'ends' of human action enjoined by Reason in its practical activity. It is a misunderstanding of Kant to think, as some apparently do, that he taught we should do our duty whatever the consequences, and without regard to goals or purposes. The misunderstanding probably arises from reading only the *Groundwork to the Metaphysic of Ethics*, without going on to read the *Metaphysic of Ethics* itself. In the latter work, Kant makes it clear that he thought there were necessary 'ends of Reason' that persons objectively ought to pursue – these ends being the happiness of others and the fullest realization of our own personal capacities.

The connection between objective obligation and an objective goal is clear. If there is something all humans ought to aim at, this is an objective purpose of human life, given, not by individual decision, but by human nature itself. But the affirmation of such an objective purpose gives a transcendental (not using this word in

Kant's technical sense) dimension to personalism. For it implies that the universal ideal of self-realization is rooted in an objective purpose, and that the universe, or human life in the universe, is in some sense purposive or directed towards a moral goal. Such a moral purpose is transcendental in the double sense that it is other than 'natural', in G. E. Moore's sense of the term – that is, wholly locatable as an object in space and time – and it is greater, or of more value than, any purely natural state.

There can be a non-religious sense of such a transcendental ideal. Iris Murdoch's Platonically influenced concept of 'the Good' may be regarded as such a non-religious sense, in that there is no cult devoted to the Good, so far as I know. But there are a number of religious interpretations. For some East Asian religions, the moral ideal is a possible state of this physical universe, when human life fully conforms to the 'Way of Heaven'. For some Buddhists, the moral ideal is liberation from the wheel of rebirth – that is a goal completely transcendent to the physical universe, though it is a possible and universal goal of human striving. For theists, the moral ideal is identical with a purpose conceived in the mind of God, creator of the universe.

In each case, the moral ideal is realizable or in some sense realized (for instance, nirvana, the state of absolute wisdom, compassion and bliss, exists, and God is a fully realized personal being), and the ideal is an objective goal of human striving. A major function of religions that use such a concept is to relate humans consciously to the ideal, to help them realize the ideal in the world, and to lead to some sort of ultimate unity with the ideal. For example, Christian practice aims to help devotees to know and love God, to realize divine love and wisdom in the world, and ultimately to attain union with the divine nature.

Not all religions are personalist in this sense. There are some religions that conceive of God as an omnipotent power that is beyond morality. Such a God can arbitrarily choose to favour some people rather than others, or can choose to destroy many people or torture them for ever if he wishes. Such a God could issue rules that humans have to obey on pain of death, or could command self-abnegation and abasement instead of human fulfilment. Such religious beliefs are not personalistic or humane. For that reason, many religious beliefs need to be moralized, to be made more consistent with our ordinary moral beliefs, and more fully aware that God is a moral ideal, the supreme Good, and not just a morally neutral or even morally callous intelligence.

When this is done, it becomes apparent that the idea of a supremely good God must be the idea of a universally benevolent God, not one who prefers one set of people to others, or who does not care about most of the world's population. And though self-denial may be part of a truly good life, such denial must be subordinated to a sense that there are many true goods to be obtained in life, and that there are many positive goods to be sought as well as evils to be avoided.

Religious beliefs, like all human beliefs, develop through time and reflection. So some early beliefs about God in the Bible, for instance, show elements of nationalism or tribal triumphalism. God is the Lord who brings victory or success to one group of people, and opposes the gods of others. But by the time of the major prophets, in the sixth to eighth centuries BCE, God is seen as the one and only creator of all peoples, who cares for the whole creation, while giving the twelve tribes a special vocation in making God's justice and compassion known.

There is no reason why such a reflective development of ideas of supreme goodness should stop with the prophets, or with the promulgation of any particular scripture. Some scriptures, like the Bible or the Qur'an, have become canonical. They mark a normative stage of development in one tradition of religious thought, and it is usually held by believers that their fundamental insights are definitive. But there still needs to be further reflection on the implications of those insights, especially as social conditions change in quite radical ways. To take the Christian tradition as an example, for

Christians it is a definitive insight into the nature of God, recorded in the New Testament, that the divine love is unlimited in extent and depth. Yet even now Christians have not managed to work out, or even agree upon, what such unlimited love requires, with regard to care for the earth, for animals and for social justice. Basic moral principles have not changed – respect for life, compassion, truthfulness, honesty, and concern for justice. But rapid advance in science and technology, and the social changes associated with them, have created a quite new set of moral problems that cannot be resolved just by appeal to those basic principles. These are problems for religious and non-religious people alike. The ancient scriptural resources of religion do not directly address them, and believers have to tease out implications or suggestions from their tradition, often rather ambiguous, that seem most relevant to current situations.

The argument of this book is that humanism or personalism – the belief that the realization of distinctive personal capacities is the highest moral ideal – is a moral advance on views of morality as obedience to allegedly authoritative rules that need have no relevance to human fulfilment. But humanism is not intrinsically anti-religious. It developed from a Judeo-Christian stress on the value of every human life as made in the image of a God of freedom, creative power, and self-giving goodness. It posits a moral goal for human life, and so it remains strongly suggestive of an objective moral purpose in the universe, and of a being (presumably intelligent and good) who could conceive such a purpose.

The God humanists do not believe in is an all-powerful tyrant who hands down unquestionable commands that often frustrate human fulfilment (in the subjugation of women, for example, or in suspicion and censorship of artistic creativity). There is, however, a God of humanism, who wills the fullest realization of the capacities of the persons whom God has created precisely to grow and flourish in the world God has made. I think that if personalism is to be a categorical moral ideal, it needs a transcendental dimension, a nonmaterial or spiritual reality that can write that ideal into the universe as an objective moral purpose, and that can enable that purpose to be realized.

In my view, what humanism has done is to further moralize the idea of God, so as to bring out more clearly what has always been implicit in the fundamental doctrine (explicitly stated in Judaism and Christianity) that God creates humans in the divine image. What religion does is enable humanism to be seen as a categorical, objective and realizable moral goal, no longer in danger of degenerating into an optional way of life for a cultural elite or a prejudiced preference for the human species.

In defence of such a religious humanism or, as I prefer to call it, transcendental personalism, I consider a number of characteristic and important moral problems in the modern world. And, by considering the Jewish, Christian, Muslim and Buddhist traditions, I try to show how these traditions contain resources for a distinctively religious and personalist approach to the problems.

There are non-personalist strands in virtually all religious traditions – as there are in almost all systems of moral belief, religious or not – and I have tried to present them fairly, while advocating the personalist alternative as both a more adequate interpretation of the traditions themselves and as more appropriate to the modern world. Transcendental personalism sees one major moral purpose of the cosmos as the fullest realization, in all personal agents, of the personal qualities of creativity, cognitive sensitivity, and communal responsibility. That formula does not solve all modern moral problems, but it creates a background view of morality in the light of which they can be reasonably addressed. It shows how religion can make a vital contribution to the quest for human fulfilment. And it shows how some religious views themselves may need to change to ensure that the contribution they make to human life and society is a positive and progressive one.

The God Gene:
The Relation of Religion and Altruism

Public opinion in Britain, at least as represented by the self-designated quality press, has moved considerably over the last few decades on the question of the relation of morality to religion. At the beginning of the twentieth century it was largely taken for granted that morality depended on religion. In a well-known debate between the lawyers H. L. A. Hart and Lord Devlin,[1] Devlin argued that the whole system of British legal and moral values depended on the basic tenets of the Christian faith. So he held that the law should continue to be based upon and to support Christian values. Hart, however, defended a secular liberal view that the law should simply seek to prevent avoidable harm, and should not protect any specific value-system. At the present time, the beginning of the twenty-first century, Britain is widely held to be a multi-cultural and multi-religious society. So no preference should be given to one religion or one set of cultural values. It looks as if Hart has won the argument, and morality is largely left as a private matter for individual or sub-groups, while public law just keeps the peace and mediates social conflicts as well as it can. But things have gone further than that. Not only have morality and religion been divorced, so that public morality is no longer thought to be based on Christian or religious values. It is often said that religion is actually a danger to morality, that it is a cause of intolerance and violence, and that morality would be

---

1 Devlin, Patrick, *The Enforcement of Morals*, Oxford: Oxford University Press, 1959, and H. L. A. Hart, *Law, Liberty and Morality*, Oxford: Oxford University Press, 1963.

better off without religion. Morality should be wholly autonomous, paying no regard to religion, which often threatens the foundations of morality.

In the following chapters, I shall be looking at various areas in which religion and morality interact – the areas of war and violence, respect for nature and for life, sex and justice. In this first chapter I want to address the question of what morality is, what its fundamental bases are, and of whether or not morality is autonomous, whether religion is a dangerous influence on morality, a necessary support for it, or just a neutral and quite different area of human life. As always in philosophy, we have to begin with matters of definition. We have to get some idea of what we mean by 'morality' and by 'religion'. That is not easy. But at least we can be fairly sure that morality is connected with human action, and with actions for which people can claim some responsibility, which they are free to do or not to do. The McNaughton rules in English law give a fairly good idea of the area with which morality is concerned. They are rules for assessing when a person is responsible for their actions. They say that a person must know what they are doing, must know the difference between right and wrong, must know that what they did was wrong (if it was), and must have been able to do otherwise.

There are all sorts of problems about whether there is a natural and universal knowledge of right and wrong, and whether anyone is ever truly free, but if I dealt with those, I would never get round to the central subject of this chapter. So I will just assume that in general reasonable people do know what sorts of things are right and wrong, and that they are free, most of the time, to decide how to act. If we accept those assumptions, then morality deals with the area of responsible action, and with generally accepted rules of right and wrong conduct.

In fact I do not think it is too difficult to get universal agreement on the sorts of acts that are right or wrong. You just have to think what sorts of things you like and dislike, and see that other beings like you will like or dislike the same sorts of things in many cases.

Anything you like will be considered by you to be good. If you like ice-cream, ice-cream will be good. However, you quickly realize that not all people like ice-cream, so this is not a universal good. It is just good for some people. However, you also dislike extreme pain, and that is bad. And in this case, virtually everyone dislikes pain. So pain is a universal evil. Every sentient being has a good reason to think it evil, and to try and avoid it. From this, it is a short step to see that acts causing pain to any sentient being are morally wrong. It is also true that acts alleviating pain or causing pleasure are morally right, or at least morally good.

There will be many complications when we come to consider complex cases. But in some very simple and very general cases, there is no difficulty in identifying acts that are morally wrong. They are acts that bring about what all rational agents would agree to be bad states, other things being equal. They will include extreme pain, frustration of desires, prevention of freedom to do what one wants, or subjection to oppressive working conditions.

Morality is related to what can be rationally desired. As Aristotle said, the 'good' is the object of rational desire.[2] And moral goods are what all beings have a good reason to desire or to avoid. This gives us the Golden Rule in its negative form as the basis of morality: Do not do to others what you would not want done to you. This rule needs no religious basis, no beliefs about supernatural beings or spiritual realities. It just needs rational reflection on universal human desires. In that sense, morality is indeed autonomous; it does not depend on religion.

The Role of Religious Belief

I may seem to have finished the chapter. But of course things are much more complicated. We can indeed see what things are good

---

2 Aristotle, *Nichomachean Ethics*, 1,1.

and bad, what acts are right and wrong, in general. They are states and acts that would be chosen or avoided by some completely impartial rational observer of the human scene. The Commandments – do not kill, do not steal, and do not lie – need no divine revelation. The main Christian tradition has always said this. 'Natural law' is the natural knowledge of right and wrong that, according to Christian tradition, God has implanted in the human mind, and it means that all people have a reasonable knowledge of what is right and wrong, whatever their religious beliefs or lack of them.[3]

The Second Vatican Council of the Roman Catholic Church stated that in such natural knowledge of right and wrong, all people have a sort of knowledge of the will of God. In obeying this will, the way of salvation is open to them: 'those who without any fault do not know anything about Christ or his Church, yet who search for God with a sincere heart and under the influence of grace, try to put into effect the will of God as known to them through the dictate of conscience . . . can obtain eternal salvation.'[4]

According to this ancient Christian tradition, all human beings have a natural knowledge of right and wrong, at least with regard to very general principles. And they also have an inborn sense that they ought to do what is right. That sense is in fact the felt pressure of the will of God, though people may not be aware of that. Even if people do not believe in God, they still have a sense of the categorical obligation of duty, a sense that some things simply ought to be done or avoided, just because they are right, and for no other reason.

That is where it gets difficult. Suppose someone commits murder. He then says, 'I know murder is morally wrong; that is, being killed is something everybody has good reason to avoid, so it is a universal evil. I know I did what was morally wrong. I was not compelled to do it. So according to the McNaughton rules I am responsible. I accept

---

3 One classic text is: Thomas Aquinas, *Summa Theologiae*, 1a 2ae, question 94.
4 The Dogmatic Constitution on the Church, *Lumen Gentium*, 16.

all that. But so what? It was still sensible of me to do it, because I would have made a great deal of money, if I had not unfortunately been caught, which was a small but acceptable risk.'

The murderer is claiming that it is not always reasonable to be moral. For what is reasonable for me to do is what pays, what increases my comfort and so on. What is moral may actually decrease my personal comfort. So being moral is not always reasonable. But we must remember Machiavelli's advice that it usually pays to make others think that we are morally upright. The best policy, then, is to seem moral, while actually breaking the moral rules when it is to my great advantage.

It sometimes seems that this is the policy of most human beings. We all know what moral rules are. For the sake of general security and the efficient functioning of society, we will probably have something like police to enforce those moral rules. And we will probably try to train children to keep them, or feel guilty when they do not do so. Then most people will behave morally, most of the time, out of a combination of fear and guilt. But really sensible people will quietly break the rules, for the sake of their own advantage, or that of their families and friends. And they will most of the time get away with it.

The crunch question is: do you secretly admire such people (it would have to be secret, or people would suspect that you were not moral or trustworthy)? Or do you feel that they are not to be admired, that they are less than human, that they are corrupt? What this question reveals is that it is not enough to have a natural knowledge of right and wrong. Some people at least think there must also be a natural sense of obligation, a sense that it is right to do your duty, even at the cost of your own life. Perhaps most of us do have such a sense, though it does not seem to be quite universal – we call people without it psychopaths, but they could also be successful criminals or even business tycoons. But how can a sense of obligation be justified?

This is where religious belief has an important part to play. For religious beliefs give an account of the role a sense of obligation, a moral sense, plays in human life. In the world, there are in fact two main religious ways of doing this. The Abrahamic traditions see moral precepts as the commands of a personal God. God has created the universe, and has created human beings for an eternal destiny of friendship with God. So human existence has a purpose, and human fulfilment lies in the realization of this purpose, which is conscious relationship to God. In view of this, the only reasonable course of life is one that leads to friendship with God. The good human life begins and ends with the love of God, and life on earth is a process of learning to love God more truly. We cannot love God without wanting to do what God wants. God tells us what God wants in the commandments, and through the natural moral law engraved in our hearts. So morality is deeply reasonable, as obedience to God, rooted in the love of God, which will lead to eternal life with God. It would be stupid not to obey the moral law. And such disobedience can only be accounted for by the deep ignorance of God that exists in the human world, and by the power of sinful desires which lead us to seek self-satisfaction before love of the Good. Such self-satisfaction is doomed to frustration.

So for the religious believer morality is not after all totally autonomous. True, we know general moral precepts without appeal to God. But we can only see why it is reasonable to obey them, and very unreasonable to violate them, when we see that they are in fact the commands of God. Without God, the sense of obligation is in danger of losing its rationale. With God, the sense of obligation expands into the most intense and fulfilling love imaginable, the love of God and all that God has made and wills to flourish.

Some Indian religious traditions provide a rather different account, which does not appeal to a personal creator. It appeals primarily to the law of karma, of cosmic justice. All that we do in life has karmic consequences. If we cause harm, then in this or some future life, harm will be caused to us. If we do good, then good will be done to us. Karma is a sort of cosmic law of equilibrium. The harm and the good we do always comes back to us. If we suffer now, it is because of harms we caused in the past. If we have a good life now, it is because of our good efforts in the past. So you should keep moral precepts because if you do not, you will suffer. Karma is the Indian equivalent of a Day of Judgement. Such cosmic judgement cannot be avoided. So again the only reasonable way to live is to obey the moral law. The sense of obligation is our instinctive knowledge of the things that will bring harm or good to us in future lives. It should be said that this is not, as it may seem at first sight, just a form of long-term prudence. It is rooted in a sense of compassion for all suffering beings, and ultimately in a desire for union with a supreme state of compassion, wisdom and bliss (nirvana). But if you ask whether it is reasonable, as well as compassionate, to follow the promptings of such a sense, the answer is that suffering will come to you and to other beings if you do not, and so the ultimate justification for moral conduct is the avoidance of suffering and the attainment of supreme bliss, for yourself as well as for others. That is certainly a strong reason for moral obedience.

Both Abrahamic and Indian religious views obviously depend on beliefs that are not widely shared in secular society. If their justifications of moral obligation are to work, there must either be a personal creator, or a cosmic law of justice and rebirth for all souls. So these justifications of a moral life depend on metaphysical beliefs that are not shared by all. What, then, of those who do not share them? Is there any real justification for living a moral life?

Sociobiological Explanations of Morality

At this point the relatively new science of sociobiology, now usually called evolutionary psychology, comes into the picture. By using the insights of Darwinian evolution, it claims to provide an account of the origin of our moral sense, and to show the limits of its justification in the modern world. Sociobiology originated with the work of E. O. Wilson, as an attempt to explain characteristics of present day human behaviour in terms of the conduciveness of such behaviour to survival in the far past.[5]

Biologists had often talked rather loosely about instincts, and agreed that much animal behaviour seemed to be instinctive, rather than learned. When ants scavenge for food, when birds build nests, or when animals hibernate, they seem to do so because of some inherited behaviour-pattern, not because they have learned to do so from their parents. Knowledge of genetics enables us to say that genes, segments of DNA molecules, contain a code for making proteins which in turn build organic bodies. Genes are passed on through inheritance, and the genetic codes build bodies of a specific sort, which behave in specific ways. Properties like eye and hair colour, height and girth, are passed on through genetic codes. So are basic behaviour patterns and tendencies to behave, feel and think in specific ways. So some people are interested in ultimate questions of why they exist, or they tend to have intense feelings of awe and reverence. Others do not. Such differences in human beings can be well explained by reference to the basic genetic codes that construct bodies with inbuilt tendencies to act and with brains that tend to think and feel in specific ways.

There is not a gene for God, in the sense that there is just one slice of DNA that makes people believe there is a God. But there probably are genes that give people a tendency to believe in transcendent realities, or to have some form of religious sensibility.

We know that belief in God is specific to some cultures and not to others. The Chinese do not seem to have it, or to regard it as very important. Arabs seem to have it in abundance. So it seems that there is a very large cultural element in religious belief. But there also seems to be an inherited element. A number of social surveys suggest that about 50 per cent of human beings have a tendency to regard worship or devotion as an important part of life, whether that devotion is directed to an ancestor, an enlightened human being or

---

5 E. O. Wilson, *Sociobiology*, Harvard University Press, 1975.

to God. If this is so, the other 50 per cent will not share such tendencies, and will not tend to be religious in that way.

There are other ways of being religious. Some believers have a very intellectual approach, some practical, some devotional, and some mystical. To the extent that these are inborn tendencies, they probably are genetically based. Just as some people are musical by nature, so some people probably are religious by nature. I am just talking about tendencies, and education or reflection or social pressure can modify natural tendencies to a great extent. But it makes good sense to say that there are genes that implant tendencies to religious thoughts and feelings in quite a large sector of the human population.

It is much the same with morality. The tendency to feel sympathy for others, or to regard obligation as categorical and objective, is probably genetically based. There is nothing much we can do about such tendencies, they are just given in human nature. They do not seem to be universal – some humans seem to lack a moral sensibility altogether. But a sense of morality seems to be even more widespread than a religious sense, and there may be a genetic link between them. This seems plausible, since the religious tendency to think of ultimate reality as in some way personal or conscious naturally coheres with the moral tendency to think that there are objective obligations or duties. The link is that if there is a spiritual supreme reality, it may well be a source of moral obligations, as humans seek to relate positively to that reality, either by helping to realize its purposes (in Abrahamic views) or by seeking to achieve union with it by setting aside purely selfish desires (in Indian traditions).

Evolutionary biologists go on to explain how such tendencies have come to be encoded in human DNA through a long process of trial-and-error in the human and pre-human past. The basic hypothesis is that various permutations of DNA arise through a natural process of mutation, and they give rise to various behavioural tendencies. In the ruthless process of natural selection, some of these behaviour patterns lead to extinction while some may be beneficial to their reproduction.

For example, if an animal has a strong tendency to run away when its young are threatened by a predator, the young are likely to get eaten, and then the genes of that animal will not be reproduced. It will die out, and all its tendencies will die with it. If, on the other hand, there is a mutation that causes the animal to protect its young by diverting the predator's attention, and it sacrifices its life for its young, then the young are more likely to survive, and the genes of that animal will be reproduced. Those genes will carry the tendency to die for one's offspring. Then, surprising though it may seem at first, the tendency to be self-sacrificing for one's family or kinship group will be propagated very successfully, while the tendency to individual selfishness will be eliminated.

Some people have been influenced by Richard Dawkins' expression 'the selfish gene'[6] to think that all natural biological processes must be selfish. That is the opposite of the truth. Dawkins asserts that to talk about genes as selfish is really just a tautology. All it says is that those genes that survive are the ones that reproduce most rapidly or most extensively. Genes are blind. As they mutate, they give rise to different sorts of animal behaviour. Some of those are eliminated, and the ones that favour the most fruitful reproduction will soon predominate in the gene pool of a species. As the example I have given shows, genes likely to be favoured are often those that produce tendencies to self-sacrificing behaviour in certain circumstances. So while evolution favours lust (which produces more offspring) and aggression (which eliminates competitors), it will also favour self-sacrifice (which protects offspring against predators) and strong social bonding (which is a better defence against predators). We might expect, then, that the natural processes of evolution will produce animals that are lustful and aggressive, but also self-sacrificing and socially co-operative, at least within limits.

---

6 Richard Dawkins, *The Selfish Gene*, London: Granada Publishing, 1978.

And this is just what humans do look like. The hypothesis seems a good one.

For evolutionary biologists, mental processes build on basic physical processes. So a tendency to self-sacrifice will come into consciousness as a feeling that this is what one ought to do. We can account for the sense of moral obligation as built on a physical behaviour-pattern that is caused by a specific genetic coding sequence. That has been selected because it proved conducive to the survival of the species in the evolutionary history of the species, perhaps millions of years ago.

There will be all sorts of genetically based mental patterns. Some will have been positively conducive to survival at a certain stage. Some will be neutral, neither good or bad for survival, but harmless enough not to have been wiped out. And some may be harmful to survival, though that harm is compensated by side-effects that are very useful – pain may be a good example of that, being apparently harmful but having the beneficial effect of warning animals of dangerous behaviour. So in the modern world we may expect that a good many humans will have a strong sense of moral obligation, though many will have genetically based tendencies to immoral actions (acts based on lust and aggression) as well, and some will lack a sense of obligation altogether. It all depends on their genes.

Is Moral Obligation an Illusion?

This account is an illuminating one. It helps to explain why humans are as morally confused as they are. But what does it say about the status of our sense of moral obligation? It is at this point that some evolutionary biologists have adopted views that seem to undermine the sense of obligation altogether. For example, the philosopher Michael Ruse, in *Evolutionary Naturalism*,[7] writes that 'morality is

---

7 Michael Ruse, *Evolutionary Naturalism*, London: Routledge, 1992.

no more . . . than an adaptation, and as such has the same status as such things as teeth and eyes and noses' (p. 241). We are not responsible for our noses. So the implication is that we are not responsible for our sense of morality either. Some people are moral and some are not, and there is nothing we can do about it. He goes on to say that the sense of oughtness is 'a collective illusion of the genes' (p. 250), and 'a better understanding of biology might incline us to go against morality' (p. 283). So if we accept evolutionary theory, we might realize that our sense of obligation is an illusion which we might do well to get rid of, if we can. Morality is no longer categorically commanding. It is the result of a million evolutionary accidents, and if it is an inconvenience, if for instance it gets in the way of our pursuit of pleasure, we might be well rid of it.

There is a sense in which Professor Ruse is correct. Some people have an over-developed sense of obligation, something of which Freud made us well aware. They might feel obligated to do things that most of us would feel are irrelevant or even absurd, like not stepping on the cracks of the pavement. In such cases, the recommendation is to replace a sense of absolute taboo, for which we can find no reason, with a course of action that can be seen to be reasonable.

We are back to reason again. But we have not avoided the problem of the two quite distinct sorts of reason – impartial reason that regards all humans, and perhaps all sentient life, as proper objects of moral concern, and prudential reason that puts the interests of ourselves and our kinship groups first. Morally serious people feel that they ought to put impartial reason before prudential reason – though it would be nice if both sorts of reason agreed, and fortunately they often do. But is that feeling just 'an illusion of the genes', which some of us have and others do not?

It seems to me that we must distinguish between a sense of obligation that is simply the feeling that we ought to do something, whether or not it can be rationally justified, and a sense of obligation to do what we can see to be reasonable because it contributes to the existence of goodness and value, to human flourishing and well-being. A rational morality is one that thinks about what makes for human flourishing. This may lead us to go against some forms of customary morality that do not seem conducive to human flourishing. But it will not be 'going against morality'. It will be seeking a more reasonable morality, one that has a rational order and structure.

The evolutionary process itself is not morally based. The processes of nature do not always aim at the morally commendable. What they favour is survival and reproduction. They have given rise to us, with the natures we have. But we can now, at least within limits, decide what we shall do with those natures. As Richard Dawkins puts it, 'We alone, on earth, can rebel against the tyranny of the selfish replicators.'[8] And Michael Ruse seeks to modify his own remarks about morality being an illusion when he says, in a later book, 'The sociobiologist is committed absolutely and completely to the genuine nature of human altruism.'[9] I am not wholly convinced by this affirmation, however. For if we think that our altruism is an accidental mental mutation that we have because it proved conducive to survival in the far past, that does not seem a positive reason to continue to be altruistic now. Perhaps we can rebel against our genetic dispositions, to some extent. If so, why should we not rebel against our disposition to believe in absolute moral obligations?

If indeed we are free, to some extent, to modify our genetic tendencies, how shall we do so? What shall we do? To that practical question, evolutionary psychology, as a descriptive discipline, offers no answer. The advice that we may seek to overcome a sense of obligation or of moral abhorrence if we can see no good reason for it, seems sound. But what constitutes a good reason?

The fundamental choice between impartial reason and prudential reason remains. I have suggested that a belief in God or in a

8 Dawkins, *The Selfish Gene*, p. 205.

9 Michael Ruse, *Can a Darwinian be a Christian?* Cambridge: Cambridge University Press, 2001, p. 195.

supremely good spiritual reality provides a positive reason for seeking the way of impartial reason. For on such a hypothesis, prudential reason will in the end be self-defeating, and the impartial good sought by moral action is an achievable goal that is in the end assured of success. Moreover, the love of the Good that religion at its best seeks to inspire entails seeking to realize goodness in many forms in the world. In this sense, religious belief provides a strong motivation for commitment to an altruistic morality.

It is not the case that there is no motivation for a purely secular, non-spiritual, person to be altruistic. My argument is not that humanistic morality cannot exist without religion. That would be false. My argument is that humanistic morality can be strengthened by religion, and that religious belief is its natural and strongest ally.

Even without any religious belief in a more-than-human spiritual reality, we could seek to modify our natures in accordance with the most satisfying values we can conceive. That means we shall seek to modify lust and aggression, and cultivate sympathy and co-operation. It is not that only some people have a moral sense, so only some people can be expected to be moral. Everyone should be moral, but those who can devise a rational morality should seek to encourage moral impulses in others, and to encourage reason to rule the passions as far as possible. Evil must be discouraged by sanctions and punishments, and good must be rewarded by marks of social esteem. Evolutionary biology, then, does not undermine morality and moral sense. It explains why we are the very mixed moral creatures we are, confused mixtures of altruism and egoism, and shows how our nature should be modified by reason in order to be shaped towards what we can rationally see to be good.

Transcendental Personalism

This may seem to be a vindication of humanism, of the belief that moral views should be based on what makes for human flourishing.

21

Religion has no essential part to play, and it may safely be left to personal choice.

To this proposal I would say yes and no. Moral views should be based on what makes for human flourishing. But religion still has an important, and I think an essential part to play. In the first part of this chapter I argued that the sense of obligation, of what impartial reason would require, is only fully compelling if we believe that there actually is an Impartial Reasoner who requires us to do what it commands (and what it commands is by definition always reasonable), and who can ensure that in the end goodness will flourish, that our moral efforts will not be in vain.

In the second part, I argued that a genetically produced tendency to believe in a supreme reality in some way personal is likely to be closely associated with a tendency to believe in moral obligation, since such an association will strengthen the sense of altruism that is conducive to the preferential survival of social animals.

In fact I suspect that the relation between religion and morality is even closer than that, and that to have a strong sense of morality is already an important part of a religious consciousness. To be a good humanist you must think that human life is important, that it has a value that makes it intrinsically worthwhile. Part of that value will almost certainly lie in the distinctive properties of human nature, properties of intellectual awareness and responsible agency. We value humans because they have a sense of continuing awareness and agency, a sense of a self that can be, and that ought to be, developed and realized, a sense of moral nobility that outweighs all considerations of purely personal pleasure or satisfaction. In short, for humanists one of the greatest human excellences is the sense of moral responsibility and obligation. But the sense of obligation is already the sense of some objective pressure, some encounter with a will greater and purer than our own, a will to the good. Sociobiologists sometimes speak as if a belief in a divine commanding will – or, to put it in a less authoritarian-sounding way, a moral ideal that attracts us simply by its intrinsic value – exists solely because it has had survival value. But no conscious agent would say that a good reason for having such a belief is that it helps the species to survive. No reasonable person would search around for beliefs that will help the species (or some set of its genes) to reproduce, and adopt the beliefs for that reason. The only good reason for accepting beliefs is that we think they are true, that they are in accordance with the facts, whether or not they help anything to survive.

In fact belief in moral obligation and in a transcendent source of such obligation would only be conducive to survival if the agents concerned really believed it. Such agents would have to have some experience that convinced them of the truth of the belief. Historically, this has been an experience of God, or of a liberated state, or of some more than physical reality (perhaps the Tao or the Way of Heaven, in non-theistic religions) that has the authority to impose obligations on humans. Without such experiences belief in the objectivity of obligation is unlikely to have survived.

Sociobiologists are in danger of putting the cart before the horse. That is, seeing that belief in objective goodness has survival value, they sometimes conclude that having survival value is the reason the belief is now accepted. Whereas it is more likely that it is because the belief has been thought to be true over many generations, on grounds of experience, that it has survival value. On the whole, beliefs that endure over generations need to have some experiential confirmation, or they fade away. It is clear that there are many differences in religious beliefs, and that not all can be equally true. But the general belief that there exists a transcendent reality of supreme value – and therefore with objective moral authority – seems common to most human cultures, and constant over thousands of years.

My argument is that the core of moral belief is a sense of objective moral obligation, a sense that it is a noble thing to pursue what is good for its own sake. That is often these days thought of as humanism. But I am proposing that the core of religious belief is some experience of a reality of supreme goodness, a goodness that objectively exists, a sense that the moral ideal actually exists. That core religious sense is the ground for the tendency to seek the good for its own sake. Such a tendency seeks greater knowledge of something supremely real, something supremely desirable and attractive, not just of a bare or abstract obligation or command.

Humanism tends to see human beings as moral agents in a morally indifferent universe, heroically alone in a noble commitment to goodness for its own sake. But humanism is under attack from within, from forces beginning to ask why we should consider moral commitment to be of special moral importance. If we wish to preserve a distinctive importance for goodness, perhaps we need a form of transcendental humanism – or, as I have suggested, a rather wider notion of transcendental personalism – that sees the moral as rooted in a transcendent dimension, in a quasi-personal or conscious reality transcending the physical world. Then we could see humans, not as accidental by-products of an indifferent physical process, but as beings whose essential nature transcends the physical, who have an inner affinity with what is beyond the physical, and whose final destiny lies beyond the physical. Humans are important, because personal and moral existence is the goal of the whole cosmic process, and human distinctiveness lies in making a creative and responsible contribution to achieving that goal.

Humanism can purify religion of its tendencies to dogmatism and intolerance, by giving a reminder that all moral action should be for the sake of good, which importantly includes human flourishing. Religion can strengthen humanism by providing a cosmic background within which moral effort makes sense, has an achievable goal, and relates human life to a supremely good reality in which true fulfilment lies.

I believe that at the present time humanism needs religion if it is not to collapse under the weight of a materialistic philosophy that denies any moral importance to human life. But religion needs humanism if it is to escape from the non-rational dogmatism that is apt to override common human values in the name of some authoritarian dogma. To establish and sustain a truly humane religion is a task for our time, and I will be exploring how, in the light of our ancient religious traditions and our new moral perplexities, that may be done.

2

Religion and Violence:
The Case of Islam and Jihad

The moral dilemmas that exist in the modern world are unprecedented in their complexity and diversity. It may seem that the ancient religious traditions of our world are unprepared to face these problems, and to some it even seems that religion stands in the way of finding an acceptable solution to such problems.

Religious traditions, however, are themselves complex and diverse, and they can offer moral resources that may be surprisingly relevant to the modern age. So I want to look at both the problems raised for some by religious traditions and at the insights that religions may bring to some of the moral issues of our day. In this way it may be possible to achieve a new understanding both of religion and of morality, and of their very varied forms of relationship. In Chapter 1 I introduced the topic of religion and morality in a general way, and spoke of the new light that evolutionary biology can throw upon the origins of religious and moral belief. Some evolutionary biologists have suggested that both moral and religious beliefs are founded on illusion, and I showed that there is little reason to accept such a negative judgement. There are, however, good reasons for thinking that both altruism and belief in a transcendent personal reality evolved naturally in human beings. I suggested that the sense of an objectively existing reality in which supreme values are realized – the sense of God – provides a strong motivation and support for altruistic moral commitment. Such a sense, especially strong in the saints and sages of religion, is the experiential basis for belief in God. Where it exists or is given credence, it provides morality with strong rational support, rooting morality in an objective reality that can be loved for its own sake, and giving human existence a moral goal. A strong sense of morality, however, is needed to monitor and interpret religious experience so that religious belief is truly conducive to ultimate human flourishing. That is my general position. But I need to examine some specific pressing moral issues to see how this might work out in detail. In this chapter I will address the topic of religion and violence. Some writers – for example, Richard Dawkins in his book *The God Delusion*[1] – have recently argued that religion is the major cause of violence and war in the world. This is a view which it is impossible to justify if one looks at human history.[2] Our history is a tragic story of violence and warfare, and religious issues have quite often been involved in wars. But by far the vast majority of wars have been fought over non-religious issues of territory, ethnic hatred, or in the pursuit of power. The first half of the twentieth century was probably the most violent period in the history of the world. More people were killed in World Wars One and Two than in the whole of the rest of human history. But those wars were not religious. The majority of conflicts that disfigure the world today are not religious. They are conflicts rooted in differences of language, culture and race. It would be surprising if religion alone escaped this violence, since religion is often associated with a particular culture or ethnic group. But the facts do not support the view that religion is the major cause of warfare.

Nevertheless, critics of religion can point out that there have been religious wars and persecutions, and that in the modern world there are groups who perpetrate violence in the name of religion. The best known are groups like Al-Qaeda, groups which claim that true Islam – that is, of course, their own version of Islam – is committed to war against all unbelievers. Such a war is a 'holy war', and its followers call it a 'jihad'. However much most Muslims protest that Islam is a

---

1 Richard Dawkins, *The God Delusion*, London: Bantam, 2006.

2 I have provided a historical overview in *Is Religion Dangerous?*, Oxford: Lion Hudson, 2006.

religion of peace, their voices are drowned out by Islamic jihadists who call on Muslims to kill unbelievers, innocent and guilty alike. Here, at least, are people whose religion promotes intolerance and violence.

What are we to make of that? How are we to explain it? Does it provide ammunition for those who say that religion is by its very nature a major cause of violence? Can there ever be a 'holy war', a war carried out in the name of God? Can the threat of violence be eliminated from religion?

Jihad

The idea of 'jihad' is central to the Qur'an, which is believed by Muslims to be the actual words of God given to Muhammad in a uniquely authoritative form of revelation – *tanzil*. In reflecting upon the Qur'anic doctrine of jihad, it is important to realize that it is positively misleading to quote texts out of context. We need to try to discern remarks about the legitimate use of violence in the context of the wider and more basic message of justice, mercy, charity and brotherhood that is the main thrust of the Qur'an.

The word 'jihad' means 'striving', and refers to striving in the way of God. This is not essentially connected with the use of force at all. But there is no doubt that Islam has a doctrine of the legitimate use of force. I will try to say what that is, and show that it is in fact part of the function of religion to help to lay down the limits of a legitimate use of force. My argument will be that the Qur'anic doctrine is very similar to the Christian doctrine of the 'just war'. Though the doctrine can be misused, it is basically concerned with the question of when the use of force is justified or required, and it places firm limits on the justifiable use of force. In the violent times in which the Prophet's mission originated, it is not surprising that the idea of jihad – 'striving in the way of God' – became important, and that it involved the idea of military conflict.

The Qur'an repeatedly calls followers to be ready for battle: 'those who believe fight in the cause of God' (4.76); assures them that death in battle is a form of martyrdom: 'If you are slain or die in the way of God, forgiveness and mercy from God are far better' (3.157); and berates those who hold back, seeking excuses not to fight: 'Those who strive and fight hath He distinguished above those who sit (at home)' (4.95). There is thus a militaristic strand in the Qur'an, and it was this strand that united the Arab tribes and led them on a campaign of conquest that was remarkably successful, extending the faith of Islam in an amazingly short time throughout the whole of the southern and eastern Mediterranean.

Because this success involved war with the Byzantine and Persian Empires, it has led some people to think that Islam is inherently a militaristic power, believing itself to have divine authority to subdue the world to the one true religion, by force if necessary. There are some Muslims who believe this. Sayyid Qutb, in his influential book, *Milestones on the Road*,[3] holds that only the Law of God, based on the Qur'an, is valid, and that Islam has a mission to establish that law, by force if necessary, throughout the whole world. This includes over-throwing all nominally Muslim governments, if they do not impose Sharia on their people, in the form in which it is found on a literal reading of the Qur'an and the Sunnah (the example of the Prophet).

The belief that Islam is the final true religion that supersedes all others, that God wills it to be for all people, and that the use of force is justified in pursuing the universal acceptance of Islam, may be thought to provide a justification for Sayyid Qutb's beliefs. This is, however, decisively not the belief of mainstream or traditional Muslims, who would regard it as an over-simple and indeed per-verse view of Qur'anic teaching. I agree with that judgement.

But before Qutb's view is condemned outright by non-Muslims, it should be remembered that Empires like that of Alexander, Rome, Persia and Britain, were established largely by force and without any

---

3 Sayyid Qutb, *Milestones on the Road*, published in English by Maktabah Publishers, 1965.

thought of establishing a divinely ordained society of justice and compassion. So it is certainly not true that Islamic imperialism is uniquely threatening to other societies. It may even plausibly be said that some subject peoples welcomed the Islamic conquests, as freeing them from greater oppression by some other imperial power. To bring justice and peace to the nations is a lofty calling, to free people from oppression is commendable, and to overthrow harsh and cruel rulers is a good cause. So jihad, even in its most militaristic forms, could be seen as a fight against tyranny and oppression, a fight indeed in the cause of God, to establish a moral, just and compassionate order and a universal brotherhood on earth.

Together with the vast majority of Muslims, I do not accept that the Qur'an in fact recommends a positive use of force to establish one specific and rather debatable view of justice throughout the world. I am simply pointing out that at least it does not, even in Qutb's version, express imperialistic expansion for the sake of it, or to exercise power for its own sake. It does aim at justice and freedom for the oppressed. There is a moral motivation present – though that motivation is corrupted by missing the more important Qur'anic teaching of compassion, tolerance and benevolence. It is corrupted by failing fully to see that jihad is primarily a spiritual principle, even when it has implications for the use of force.

For Muslims, there are always important spiritual principles underlying the specific admonitions of the Qur'an. But those principles need to be drawn out by a process of reflection, discussion, and reference to precedents, in the light of many other relevant texts from the Qur'an, and of the very different conditions under which Muslims in different societies live. In this way a scholarly consensus is sought, but it is generally recognized that a number of variant schools of Islamic jurisprudence can coexist.

It is not difficult to interpret jihad spiritually. Since it means 'striving', it need not refer to war – though it undoubtedly does in many Qur'anic verses. It can refer to spiritual striving to serve God in the way of justice and compassion – after all, Allah is repeatedly said to be just, merciful and forgiving, and it is repeatedly said to be better to forgive than to exact the permitted penalty.

One verse expresses such a thought particularly well – 'Those who believe and suffer exile and strive with might and main in God's cause, with their goods and their persons, have the highest rank in the sight of God' (9.20). To strive with one's possessions and by using one's gifts in the cause of God, even in conditions of exile or oppression, in the cause of justice, truth, kindness and benevolence, is jihad in the fullest spiritual sense. This sense of jihad is an internal striving, exerting oneself to further the purposes of God.

But there is a second sense of jihad. We can strive in competition with others to be more just and merciful, more devoted to the love of God, more given to prayer and gratitude to the creator of all things. 'To each is a goal to which God turns him. Then strive together (as in a race) towards all that is good' (2.148). Often the Qur'an sees different religions as opportunities for this sort of striving rather than for armed conflict. 'If God had so willed, he would have made you a single people . . . therefore strive in all virtues' (5.51). In a mysterious way, God does not will that all should agree in religion, and differences in faith can be opportunities for 'striving in virtue', for seeking to excel in justice and mercy. This sense of jihad, too, does not involve the thought of violent conflict.

There is, however, a third sense of jihad, which may involve the use of legitimate force. But it is not the case that Islam has a mission to exterminate other religions. The Qur'an clearly states, 'Let there be no compulsion in religion' (2.256). True belief cannot be compelled. Attacks by force on Islamic faith should be resisted by force: 'If any do help and defend themselves after a wrong (done) to them, against such there is no cause for blame' (42.41). Even so, the chapter immediately continues, 'but if any show patience and forgive, that would truly be an exercise of courageous will' (42.43).

The traditional doctrine of war in Islam is that believers have a right to defend themselves against attack. The basic rule is the law of retaliation – 'Recompense for an injury is an injury equal' (42.40).

And again the qualifying clause follows at once – 'But if a person forgives and makes reconciliation, his reward is due from God.' These verses refer primarily to personal injuries, but can be reasonably extended to cover relations between states. There are limits on the conduct of war, that must not be transgressed – 'Fight in the cause of God those who fight you, but do not transgress limits' (2.190). And there is a place for forgiveness and reconciliation. Nevertheless, once a war of defence has begun, Muslims should commit themselves unreservedly to it.

'Fight then on until there is no more tumult or oppression, and there prevail justice and faith in God' (2.193). 'Seize them and slay them wherever you find them, and take no friends or helpers from their ranks' (4.88). These two texts have been used by critics of Islam to show that Muslims believe in total war against unbelievers. But such phrases must not be taken out of context. Each verse is immediately followed by an important qualification. After the first, comes the sentence, 'But if they cease let there be no hostility except to those who practice oppression.' And after the second, 'if they withdraw from you but fight you not and (instead) send you (guarantees of) peace, then God hath opened no way for you (to war against them)'. It seems clear that the Qur'an does not license wars of conquest in general, and that the moral limits on warfare are very much the same as those that developed in Christianity in the Middle Ages.

In the thirteenth century, Thomas Aquinas held that a justified war must be declared by a sovereign, must have a just cause (either self-defence or defence of the weak and oppressed), and must have a realistic prospect of success. In the sixteenth century, de Vitoria added that war must be waged by proper means, and must be discriminate (not directly killing the innocent) and proportionate (using minimal force to achieve a good end). War is justified in self-defence, but the virtues of compassion and reconciliation should never be forgotten. Attempts should be made to discriminate between active combatants and innocent bystanders, the use of force should be the minimum necessary and must bring about more good than harm – and there must be a reasonable hope of victory. The jurists of Islam agree almost completely with these principles, and so military jihad and the Catholic 'just war' tradition are almost identical. It follows that there is no reason to see Islam as more violent or militaristic than the main Christian tradition.

Hard Verses in the Qur'an

Yet it is undeniable that modern Islam has a particular problem with violence. There are groups advocating indiscriminate slaughter just for the sake of creating terror, which give themselves names like 'Islamic Jihad'. This is a major problem for Islam, and it does stand in need of some explanation.

In beginning to address the issue it is important to recognize that the origins of Christianity and Islam are quite different. Christianity began as a small Jewish movement devoted to non-violence, in a province of the Roman Empire. It was only when it became the official religion of that Empire, in AD 395, that the religion had to consider questions of war and the use of force. Islam began as a reform movement in Arabia, and from the first it sought to unite the Arabic tribes in a socio-political union, in face of violent opposition. Muhammad was a social and military leader, and so rules for warfare are integral parts of the Muslim scripture in a way that is not true of the New Testament. It is very important to know the context in which these rules were first promulgated, and it is unfortunately easy for those who pay little attention to the juridical history of Islam, or who ignore the original contexts of specific Qur'anic revelations, to provide deviant interpretations.

The best known cases are from Chapter 9 of the Qur'an, where you can find the texts, 'Fight and slay the pagans wherever you find them' (9.5) and 'Fight those who believe not in God nor the Last Day, nor hold that forbidden which has been forbidden by God and his apostle, nor acknowledge the religion of truth (even if they are) of the People of the Book, until they pay the *jizya* [the tax on non-Muslims in Muslim states] with willing submission, and feel themselves subdued' (9.29). Taken out of context, these passages could license war on all polytheists or non-theists, and the imposition of Muslim law on all non-Muslims. Sayidd Qutb does interpret them in that way. But chapter 9 deals with the question of what is to be done when an enemy with whom a treaty has been made breaks faith and is guilty of treachery. The general teaching of the chapter is that there should first be a breathing space of four months to allow for repentance and reconciliation. After that, the first quotation enjoins war – but the fuller text prohibits war against pagans with whom a treaty remains in force (9.4), and it continues, 'If they repent and establish regular prayers and practise regular charity, then open the way for them.' There is no licence for war against those who co-exist in peace with Muslim states.

The second quote also applies only to people who have 'violated their oaths, plotted to expel the Apostle, and were aggressors by being the first (to assault) you' (9.13). Most traditional commentators note that the religious tax on non-Muslims is a nominal one, signifying that non-Muslims are content to live in a Muslim state in peace. So the call to fight in the cause of God is a call to fight only against those who are actively hostile to Islam.

The general teaching of the Qur'an is that if people are not convinced by the superiority of Islam, then the issue must be left to God, not decided by force of arms. Indeed, to impose Islam by force might be seen as self-defeating, since true Islam is submission of the heart to God, and that cannot be compelled. The traditional Islamic view is therefore that, while forces that make Islamic practice impossible or that are actively hostile to Islam must be opposed – and that is part of jihad – Muslims should live in peace with others who are not hostile.

History of Islamic Empires

The history of Islam has seen the faith readjusting to very different sets of conditions, and that history underlies the self-understanding of many Muslims in the modern world. The first two phases of Islamic history were of victory and expansion, giving Islam a sense of world mission and manifest destiny. The religion expanded at an amazing rate in the first few years of its existence, largely through military prowess. In its first stage, Muhammad was opposed by many tribes, and some chapters of the Qur'an are marked by the command to fight and defeat the enemies of the Prophet, that is those who wished to exterminate the new faith and restore old tribal traditions. Islam was victorious, and the Arab tribes rejected their polytheistic cults and united around the religion of the Prophet.

In a second stage, which followed very quickly, Arab forces over-ran almost the whole of the Byzantine Empire, eliminating it in the African continent, establishing flourishing cultures in Al Andalus (Spain), Baghdad and the old Persian Empire, and Damascus in the Eastern Mediterranean. It must have seemed as though Islam was destined to spread throughout the world. Western Europe, after the collapse of the Western Roman Empire, was in the Dark Ages, and the Byzantine Empire, seen as corrupt and tyrannical by its subject peoples, who asked the Arab forces for help, was in decay. Turks and Mongols, who had their own programme of imperial expansion, converted to the new faith, and this led to the creation of vast Muslim empires. The world lay at the feet of Islam, or so it seemed.

Then the world changed. At first, Islam was helped by the fact that potentially powerful opponents, Byzantium and Persia, were weakened by their own conflicts. The Berbers, Mongols and Turks converted to Islam, and so became allies rather than enemies. But, like all Empires, the Islamic world began to fragment internally. The Islamic empires deprived the Caliph of political power in AD 945. The three great Muslim empires, the Ottoman, the Persian and the

Mughal Empire in India, became involved in religious and political strife, between Shi'a and Sunni Islam and between different imperial contenders for domination. And from the fourteenth century on, Europe began to emerge as a new vital world civilization. As vast areas of the world were colonized by European Christian nations, Muslim states began to decline culturally and politically. The growth of modern science and technology in Europe after the seventeenth century led to the European colonization of the world, and in particular of the Islamic nations. They did not participate in this scientific advance, even though some of them had been at the forefront of early medieval science, when Europe was still in the Dark Ages. So the third stage of Islamic history was one of decline and defeat, epitomized by the abolition of the Ottoman dynasty and the abolition of the Caliphate in 1924. At the nadir of Muslim political fortunes, however, European colonialism too began to collapse. As Muslim countries freed themselves from colonial control, this left a sense of resentment against the colonial powers that still smoulders. Traditional Muslim rulers are seen by some as the tools of Western imperialism. The creation of the secular state of Israel in 1948 was widely seen by Muslims as a continuation of Western colonization, and subsequent interventions in Afghanistan and Iraq can easily be interpreted as attacks on the self-determination of Muslim nations.

In such a context, jihad can be and has been reactivated in some quarters as a military defence of Islam, under attack by Western imperialism. But in fact the situation in the modern world is much more complex that such over-simple analyses suggest. Regrettably, the Islamic world is still divided in many ways – into Shi'ite and Sunni, into traditionalist, modernizing and militant, into broadly secular and conservatively religious, and into various ethnic groups. Where jihad can still be interpreted as a defence of the 'true faith' under attack from 'hypocrites' or 'infidels', where relatively undeveloped countries feel themselves exploited by more dominant economic powers, where national governments are unstable or inefficient or both, and where those governments are felt to be under undue foreign influence, Islam can become a force for violent conflict. This is a special geopolitical context, in which centuries of hostility and misunderstanding still have to work themselves out. But the old world of competing empires is in fact already dead, and the global society in which we all now live poses quite a new set of opportunities and also problems. We are living at a time when the sad legacy of past violence is still at work, but when the future is already ushering in quite a new world order.

The New World Order

The root religious cause of much violence in parts of the Muslim world – in Islamic Jihad and in Muslim insurgencies in many countries, for instance – is the difficulty some believers have in accepting a pluralistic and humane interpretation of Islam, open to interaction with a wide variety of intellectual and cultural influences. Yet just such an interpretation was the dominant one in the 'golden age' of Islam, up until the fourteenth century. In Spain (Al Andalus), when Muslim culture was at its height, Muslims, Jews and Christians lived together, admittedly under Muslim oversight, but still in a greater degree of tolerance than medieval Christians managed to show. Islamic culture was sophisticated and philosophically astute, welcoming philosophers like Ibn Rushd (Averroes) and Ibn Sina (Avicenna), who carried on the traditions of Greek philosophical reflection. From the very beginning there were variant interpretations of Islam, and proclamation of the Faith was held to be important precisely because it brought unity between warring tribes, and because it taught devotion to goodness rather than tribal self-interest and personal egotism, and acceptance of diversity rather than cultural oppression. It is ironic that even militant jihadists tend to look back upon that time with reverence and regret for its loss. If Islam is true to its highest expressions of its essential identity, a recovery of that tolerant, humane and open attitude is indicated, and such a recovery is possible in the modern world.

The sort of unity Islam is meant to bring has always included a variety of interpretations that coexist in peace. The Faith is not based on, nor does it inculcate, hatred of others or the demonization of those who differ. On the contrary, it teaches the brotherhood of all men (we might now prefer to say the unity of all people) and the coexistence of all who are prepared to live in peace. Any hope of resolving present disputes within the Islamic world rests with the growth of such a tolerant, reconciling and humane Islam, and therefore with the emphatic recognition that these, not hatred and violence, are the central teachings of the Qur'an.

Islam has seen a new resurgence in the late twentieth century. In a newly globalized world, America has become the major global power. Europe, China, Russia, South America, Africa, India and East Asia form distinct socio-economic units alongside the block of Islamic states. But most of the non-Muslim states contain significant Muslim minorities, and Islam is now the second largest religious group in the world after Christianity, with something in excess of one thousand million adherents, and it is vital and growing, especially in Africa, Asia and Europe. The consequence is that many Muslims in the modern world live in a religious diaspora, not in Muslim states. In this new world, the situation is almost as far removed from the tribal society of the Prophet's Arabia as can be imagined. The political and social world in which Islam now exists requires a new application of laws that were given for a tribal pre-scientific society, and a new understanding of the spiritual principles that underlie those laws. In the modern world, it has become clear that any form of imperial expansion or any attempt to impose one ideology on the whole world, is highly dangerous. Warfare is still regrettably a major feature of human existence – the Brookings Institution of New York recorded 127 wars (very few of them religiously motivated, incidentally) in the 30 years after the end of World War Two, wars in which an estimated 23 million people were killed or wounded. Modern weapons now make the slaughter of the innocent virtually inevitable, and the existence of nuclear and biological weapons makes it possible for humans, for the first time in history, to exterminate all life on earth.

In this situation, it has become vital to find alternatives to war as a way of settling disputes or of establishing one socio-political system. We are not talking about establishing unity among warring Arabian tribes, and setting in place an order of justice and compassion among constantly bickering and untrustworthy social groups. However, it might well be said that we are still doing a rather similar thing on a global scale – seeking to establish unity and justice among quarrelsome, self-interested and competing nations. But that cannot now be done by fighting a few decisive battles, and putting in place a social order which all people of good will can see to be just. Already the collapse of the great Muslim empires shows that size makes a crucial difference. The attempt to unite diverse ethnic and ideological groups in one universal order is vastly unlikely to succeed. The best hope is to find some form of coexisting alliance where differences are accepted, and an effort is made to find and co-operate in positive points of agreement.

In such a world, Islam can make a reasonable claim to be primarily and in its deepest intention a religion of unity – the unity of God, the brotherhood (or, more inclusively, the unity) of all humanity under God, proclaiming the eternal significance of moral striving, and the final goal of all life in God, the supreme Good.

Interestingly, in this respect it is very like the liberal Christianity of late nineteenth-century German theologians such as von Harnack. But the criticism made of von Harnack was that he had omitted all the distinctive doctrines of Christianity – the divinity of Christ, the Trinity, and the Atonement. So an unfriendly critic might say that this version of Islam omits the distinctive doctrines of submission to the Prophet, suppression of all polytheism and atheism, and literal acceptance of the laws of the Qur'an.

What does Islamic Law Require?

There are versions of Islam that have a very exclusive view of faith. These more rigorous versions can call in aid texts like 49.15: 'Only those are Believers who have believed in God and his apostle, and have never since doubted, but have striven with their belongings and their persons in the cause of God.' For such a view, 'God is an enemy to those who reject faith' (2.98), and faith is taken to be acceptance of the Qur'an as divinely revealed: 'We have sent down to thee manifest signs and none reject them but those who are perverse' (2.99). Acceptance of the Qur'an is taken to entail acceptance of Shari'a laws like those requiring flogging with 100 lashes for adultery or cutting off hands for theft. It may be overlooked that four witnesses are required of adulterous acts, and that thieves can be forgiven if they repent and make amends (5.42). Such an exclusivist view of Islam still does not justify aggressive violence against those non-Muslims who agree to live in peace with Islam. But it is easy to see how it can give rise to campaigns of violence by those who feel themselves, however implausibly it may seem to most observers, to be under attack from enemies of Islam.

On the other hand, there are more pluralist versions of Islam that are still rigorously Islamic, but interpret 'faith' much more widely, as faith in the sovereignty of good and in the value of human striving for good. Such a wider definition of faith is suggested by the repeated Qur'anic assertion that there is just one common faith present in all societies in some form – 'We believe in God, and the revelation given to us, and to Abraham, Ishmael, Isaac, Jacob, and the tribes, and that given to Moses and Jesus, and that given to all prophets from their Lord . . . we make no difference between one and another of them, and we bow to God' (2.136). Interpreted narrowly, the claim that Abraham, Moses and Jesus all taught the same faith in detail is implausible, even if the records of their teaching are held to be imperfect or corrupted in some way. But on a broader interpretation, the faith of Abraham was faith in the God whom he knew, who called for his loyalty. So we may well think that there is a common core doctrine among many religious teachers (prophets) in many religious traditions, which is a striving to overcome egoistic desire, and to be one with a reality of wisdom, compassion and bliss – that is spiritual jihad. Then to have faith will be to be true to the revelation of supreme goodness that has come in one's own tradition.

This interpretation seems to be confirmed by the often quoted passage concerning the People of the Book: 'Those who follow the Jewish scriptures, and the Christians and the Sabians – any who believe in God and the Last Day, and work righteousness, shall have their reward with their Lord . . . on them shall be no fear, nor shall they grieve' (2.62 and 5.72). In thinking about Islam in the modern world, theologians have to consider what the modern analogies are to the People of the Book. After all, there are vast civilizations in China and India that have no 'Book' and no prophets in the Qur'anic sense. Yet they have ancient religions and religious teachers, they have high standards of moral conduct, and they teach a spiritual striving in the way of goodness – whether it is the *sanatana dharma* (the eternal way) of India or the Tao of China.

Perhaps a Muslim can apply to them the saying, 'To every people have we appointed rites and ceremonies, which they must follow' (22.67). It seems clear that they should be invited to Islam, but not compelled to submit. After that, the issue lies with God: 'If it had been God's plan, they would not have taken false gods: but we made thee not one to watch over their doings, nor art thou set over them to dispose of their affairs' (6.107). If people conscientiously choose different paths, the Muslim may say, 'To you be your Way and to me mine' (109.6). At the resurrection God will make clear who was correct, but until that time, conscientious difference must be accepted.

Forms of Islam

Islam originated in a situation of social conflict, in which it had to fight for its existence against hostile tribes. It succeeded in building a strong and united society in Arabia. Then it rapidly extended its rule throughout the known world, largely by force of arms, as old Empires crumbled and as new imperial powers converted to Islam and established further great empires. Among some people this has given it the reputation of being essentially a militant faith, a reputation consolidated by many situations in the modern world in which there are a number of militant – self-styled jihadist – Muslim organizations. These organizations, however, are forced to reject traditional Islam, with its insistence on the need for a fourfold root of faith – the Qur'an, the Sunnah or traditions of the life of the Prophet, the consensus of scholars, and analogy as a principle of applying the law to new situations. Traditional Islam is wholly opposed to uses of Qur'anic texts that ignore the well-established scholarly traditions of interpretation, and that act as though violence was still a possible route to world peace. Traditional Islam itself is divided (though not violently) between those who think that the 'door of *ijtihad*, of private interpretation' was closed at a fairly early time in Muslim history, probably in the fourteenth Christian century, and those who allow for new interpretations not bound by such ancient precedents. There are also divisions between those who support the view that Muslim states should implement Shari'a, in some form, as state law, and those who accept the necessity for a broadly secular, or non-aligned, law for the state, with Shari'a largely governing certain matters of family or religious law.

All these divisions exist within a generally traditional form of Islam, and help to clarify the sense in which any form of global Islam must be a diversity-in-unity. It cannot plausibly and does not usually seek the unrealizable ideal of a monolithic and universal state. Traditionalist Muslims stress that at heart Islam was always a movement for spiritual and moral reform, for submission to a God of justice and mercy, and to a just and charitable social order. If we think of jihad as striving in the cause of goodness, and think of the invitation to Islam as an invitation to a universal human fellowship that co-operates in such striving, we might discern the real heart of Islam.

There will probably always exist a rigorist form of Islam, stressing obedience to Shari'a exactly as described in the Qur'an, and accept-ance of the finality of the Qur'an. But even the most rigorist forms will not find Qur'anic justification for religious wars of aggression and conquest. And they will have to accept their status as minority interpretations within the wider spectrum of Islamic faith.

For most traditionalist Muslims greater stress is placed on the basic principles of unity, tolerance and justice. More flexible inter-pretations of Shari'a, less wedded to the letter of ancient customs and more keenly aware of the minority and diasporal status of Islam in a pluralist but globally connected world, exist. It can still be true that 'This is no less than a message to (all) the worlds' (38.87). But the message will be one of submission to goodness, striving for goodness and the unity of all in fellowship, and hope for the fulfilment of all life in God. For such views, the vocation of Islam may be more to influence the whole world for good than to include all people within its own household.

Most traditional scholars stress the importance of the fact that the Qur'an was recited in various stages, its 114 chapters being 'sent down' over a period of 23 years. The first stage was at Mecca, where the preaching of the Prophet aroused opposition so great that after 13 years he moved to Medina (known as the *hijra*, beginning the Muslim calendar and traditionally dated to the Christian year AD 622). His followers were subject to attack by various groups of Jews, Christians and by the Meccan Arabs. But Muhammad formed a military force strong enough to subdue all opposition in Mecca, and returned there for the last two years of his life. Since the Qur'an was addressed to the Prophet's Arabic followers in a time of military conflict, it is natural that many of its chapters relate to specific, and changing, conditions in Mecca and Medina, and the emphases of the Meccan and Medinan chapters tend to be different. Furthermore, the order of chapters in the Qur'an as we have it is not the order in which they were received by the Prophet, and so a good deal of scholarship is needed to place particular chapters in specific contexts.

The context may make a great deal of difference, for example, in remarks made about relations with Jews and Christians, the 'People of the Book'. Sometimes the Christians were friendly, but sometimes they were hostile, and these differences gave rise to differing recommendations about Muslim relations with them. Thus there are statements like, 'Nearest among men in love to the Believers wilt thou find those who say: we are Christian' (5.85), possibly referring to the Abyssinian Christians who supported Muslim refugees during the time of their persecution in Mecca. But there are also statements like, 'Take not the Jews and Christians for your friends' (5.54), promulgated when Christians had colluded with the enemies of the Prophet. It is difficult to generalize such remarks to very different times and situations. In Muslim tradition a doctrine of 'abrogation' has developed, in accordance with which scholars hold some texts to be abrogated by others, either because the abrogating texts are later in time, or because they apply to a wider set of circumstances, or because they penetrate more deeply to the heart of the Prophet's message, which may on some specific occasions have had to be temporarily qualified or set aside because of some historical difficulty.

Clearly scholars may disagree on which texts abrogate others, and on the precise reasons for abrogation. Yet there is here a decisively important point that the texts need interpretation by those who have a good knowledge of their original contexts and of the traditions of scholarly reflection in succeeding centuries. A good theological education in Islam will try to inculcate wise principles of interpretation and a sensitivity to what lies at the heart of the Qur'an, and what belongs to particular contexts of its promulgation that have changed in fairly basic ways. The spirit of discernment is needed for understanding the message of God as it applies to rapidly changing situations.

The message remains unchangeable. But its application to new circumstances requires discrimination and wise judgement. Legal and religious scholarship are, for most Muslims, essential for interpreting the Qur'an, and where that is the case, discussion and personal judgement are always an important part of religious life. It is irresponsible to take texts out of context, and read them at face value. This is why it is vital to remember that the Qur'an is not a book of clear and straightforward rules, to be applied without much regard for social circumstances. It is the teaching of God for finding the path to Supreme Goodness, but that path needs to be discerned by the prayerful community, seeking to share in the mind of God as it is definitively expressed in the Qur'an.

Beyond traditionalist Islam, as I have described it, there are various modernist or liberal movements that accept the applicability to the Qur'an of the methods of critical history, the need fully to accept the best findings of modern science, the necessity of working out specific moral rules on the basic Qur'anic principle of human fulfilment in God, the Supreme Good, and the importance of defending freedom of conscience in religion. These movements may seem particularly well suited to a rapidly changing, essentially pluralistic and strongly interconnected world.

Such humane and pluralist views are perfectly consistent with belief that the Qur'an is indeed the inerrant revelation of God to the Prophet, and that it will not be superseded by any subsequent inspired prophecy of the same sort. All that is required is that the verses of the Qur'an are placed in their historical contexts, and that its underlying principles are discerned and applied in new contexts, as what is believed by Muslims to be the final prophetic revelation is understood in the light of new scientific knowledge about both physical and human nature, and in a more global context.

If the right of private interpretation is granted, the danger of more intolerant interpretations cannot be wholly eliminated, but the best hope of avoiding them is to stress the prime importance of spiritual jihad, a striving for goodness which avoids all hatred and seeks always the sovereignty of good. Islam is still seeking its proper role in a world in which it will for the foreseeable future exist largely as a minority faith. Globally speaking, it will probably always only encompass a minority of the human race. But to the extent that it motivates a striving in the way of supreme goodness, a striving for justice among all people and a striving to show effective compassion for the poor of the earth, Islam can be a great force for good in the world, an *umma* called to be an example of mercy and devotion to the supreme Good.

The doctrine of jihad is central to Islam. It is a dangerous doctrine in the hands of those who believe that a system of religious law should be imposed on everyone by force. But at the heart of Islam there is a very different view. Jihad may need to take military expression, when and only when it is in defence of the oppressed and those who are unjustly attacked. But it is primarily and above all the spending of one's person and possessions in striving for that which God wills above all, the submission of one's whole self to the sovereignty of the good. This is, I think, the striving that the Qur'an seeks to evoke in its hearers. It is something that all people of good will can respect and honour, and it is in my view the distinctive witness and vocation of Islam in the contemporary world.

Conclusion

Violence is a major human problem. It disfigures the whole of human history. But it springs, not from religion, but from the hatred, greed and self-deceit that religion exists to combat. The doctrine of jihad is a doctrine of inner striving to replace hatred by compassion, greed by charity, and self-deceit by true self-knowledge. Such striving will not always succeed, and religion itself may be corrupted by those who use it to evoke hatred of those different from themselves, a desire to impose one set of beliefs on the world by force, or who foster a deluded belief that they are exclusively favoured by God. It is nevertheless religion that contains the antidote to its own corruption, and the corruption of all human life, by teaching God's universal compassion and the need to respect all God's creation.

Islam teaches that violence must always be justified by its use to protect the innocent and maintain a just and compassionate society. It must always be limited by compassion and mercy. It must never spring from or inflame hatred. Violence must sometimes be used to protect the weak and oppressed of the world, for there is in the world a real battle of good against evil. But for that reason we need to be very careful that we are not harming and oppressing when we mean to protect freedom and human flourishing. Jihad should always be a striving in the way of God, who is the compassionate, the merciful, and the just, and who cares for the flourishing of all creation.

That is the basic teaching of Islam – justice and not oppression, compassion and not cruelty, benevolence and not hatred. If in the world today there are Muslim groups that seem to undermine this teaching, we all need to enquire into the factors that have allowed such corruptions to thrive. Such an enquiry, if undertaken seriously and diligently, may leave us all feeling uncomfortable. But one thing we can do is try to see Islam, not through the eyes of its corrupters and detractors, but through the eyes of those who find in it the call of God to seek justice and mercy and to devote their lives, their persons and possessions, to the service of that which is supremely good.

3

Interfering with Nature:
Natural Law and Evolution

The year 1953 marked a decisive turning point in human history. In that year the structure of DNA, the mechanism of heredity, was discovered. Since then the complete human genome, the sequence of genes that determine major human bodily and mental characteristics, has been decoded. In this century, humans for the first time have the ability to identify and change the genes that make us human, that decide our characters and abilities as humans. In a completely unprecedented way, we can begin to remake human nature, and shape it in accordance with our wishes.

This raises a whole series of new moral questions that could never have arisen in this way in past history. If we have the ability to change human nature, should we do so, and in what way? There are already societies in existence that look forward to the creation of trans-humans, beings so much more intelligent, healthy and strong than us that they will be like gods, with vast power, knowledge, and perhaps even immortality.

This sounds like science fiction, but most geneticists accept that we may be able to eliminate some major heritable diseases, like cystic fibrosis, by replacing the genes that cause such conditions. This is sometimes known as negative genetic engineering. We should also be able to identify genes for such things as blonde hair, blue eyes, gender and intelligence. We may then be able to insert such genes into a sequence of genes, a genome, and produce healthy and intelligent children, of desired sex and skin-colour, to order. So it is not completely fantastic to suppose that we may be able one day to engineer a genome for a trans-human race, one that is as far superior to present humans as humans now are to chimpanzees. This is the future to which the Trans-Human Society looks forward.

At the other end of the moral spectrum are those who say that we should not tamper with the human genome at all. We should not, they say, 'play God'. Research into human genetic material is morally forbidden, because it involves experimentation on living human material. We may be able to remedy some gross genetic defects, but we should not try to change human nature itself, which is as it is meant to be.

These are perplexing moral issues, which there is no precedent for resolving. Where do the religions stand on such issues? Is genetic engineering morally permissible? And should we look forward to the replacement of the human race by a superior, artificially engineered, species?

Natural Inclinations

I have said that there is no precedent for resolving these issues. But that is not strictly true. For there is a long Christian tradition of moral thinking, partly drawn from ancient Stoic philosophy but developed in the late Middle Ages by theologians such as Thomas Aquinas, that makes a close connection between morality and human nature. For this tradition, knowledge of morality is not dependent on revelation. Its main precepts are knowable by reason, reflecting on the natural inclinations of human nature. There is thus a 'natural', non-revealed, knowledge of right and wrong. Moreover, there are some goods, or valued states, that are 'natural', in being virtually universally agreed by all rational human beings, and in being rooted in human nature.

Aquinas's version of natural law holds that the moral goods that are 'natural' are those 'towards which man has a natural tendency' or natural inclination (*naturalem inclinationem*).[1] Agreeing with Aristotle, he thinks that all things have a natural inclination to their proper end. For Aquinas, that is part of the natural order of things, as created by God. And God 'commands us to respect the natural order and forbids us to disturb it'.[2] So we should always respect, and never frustrate, our natural inclinations, and the order of nature.

A distinction needs to be made between natural inclinations, in this sense of inherent tendencies to act, and rationally desirable courses of action. In Chapter 1 I held that a good basis for morality can be found by reflecting upon the sorts of things that all people could rationally desire, or that all people would find to be undesirable from an impartial or universal point of view. This could form the foundation of a natural and universal moral law. But it is not quite what Aquinas is proposing. He thinks that God has so created all things that they have inherent natural purposes (final causes, or that for the sake of which they exist). He wants to found a natural moral law on the natural purposes of human existence as such, and proposes to find them in the natural inclinations of humans, which have been implanted by God.

This appeal to inherent final causes, or natural inclinations, is quite different from an appeal to rationally and universally desirable actions. Natural inclinations are not necessarily things that we find to be rationally desirable. I may have a natural inclination to do undesirable things. In fact I probably do, if I have a natural tendency to kill my rivals. Such inclinations may be implanted in me genetically, but they are hardly universally desirable – my rivals could not desire them, for a start.

I may also desire to do things for which there is no natural inclination. Many people desire to change their bodies by plastic surgery, even to grow facial whiskers in order to look like cats. There is no natural tendency to do that. I may have an instinctive, or

---

1 Thomas Aquinas, *Summa Theologiae*, 1a 2ae, question 94, article 3.
2 Augustine, *Contra Faustum*, Book 22, chap. 27.

natural, tendency to run from wild animals. But perhaps I should counteract that tendency, to become more courageous or in order to make friends with animals. As G. E. Moore argued, one cannot assume that a way in which I naturally tend to behave is desirable, either for myself or for others. Humans tend to rape, kill and lie, and such behaviour is very undesirable. The view that natural inclinations are, as such, good would be widely denied by evolutionary biologists. We now know, though we have only really known since the structure of DNA was discovered, that there are behavioural tendencies in human beings that are laid down in the coding of transmitted DNA.

It is our DNA that carries a code for building proteins that will in turn construct bodies with specific physical characteristics and tendencies to behave in certain 'instinctive' ways. These are our natural inclinations. In every generation DNA is subject to mutations or chemical changes – humans generate about 100 mutations per generation. Some of these are harmful, and so are anything but good. Some of them give rise to natural inclinations that may or may not be harmful. Most of the harmful inclinations are eliminated by natural selection, but some get through. So the tendency to hate foreigners, and for men to subjugate and rape women, are tendencies that may have proved quite conducive to human survival as a species. But they could hardly be called good, or in accord with the purposes of God.

It is, of course, true that the things we naturally tend to do have been conducive to survival over thousands or millions of years. Otherwise we would not have survived. And it seems likely that behavioural tendencies conducive to survival would generally have come to be thought desirable, and to be associated with pleasure. But these are not necessary or inviolable connections. I may have a tendency to take intoxicating substances, which give pleasure. Such a tendency may be genetically ingrained, and it may have survived in the genome simply because its harmfulness has not been bad enough to wipe the human species out. Nevertheless, intoxicating substances may be very bad for me, and kill me in the end. From an evolutionary point of view, this would not matter very much, since in the end I would be beyond reproductive age in any case, so the harm done to me would not cause any decrease in fecundity. It might even increase my fecundity when I am young, though it will kill me as soon as I am past child-bearing age. So this natural tendency will be good for reproductive success, but bad for me personally. If I can take rational control of my behaviour, I might well desire to live longer and reproduce less, in which case my rational desires will conflict with my natural inclinations.

To take another case, humans may be naturally aggressive, for that has had an evolutionary advantage in the past. But now it is counter-productive, and may lead to the extermination of the human race. What is genetically programmed, according to evolutionary biologists, is what was good for the survival of my genes in the far past, or what at least was not counter-productive, thousands or millions of years ago. That may now be very bad for survival, and so should be rationally opposed.

The evolutionary theorist Richard Dawkins speaks of human ability to rebel against 'the tyranny of the selfish replicators'.[3] On most evolutionary accounts, my inherited tendencies need to be rationally controlled or even opposed, for as Tennyson wrote, 'Nature is red in tooth and claw'.[4] T. H. Huxley, in a famous essay on evolution and ethics, held that evolutionary success depends on increasing lust and aggression and on the ruthless extermination of rivals.[5] The behaviour this naturally gives rise to is a strong sense of kin-group, limited altruism, coupled with extreme hostility to all competing groups. In the modern world we may need to counter these natural tendencies, extend human sympathy more widely, and encourage rational control of instinctive behaviour. Reason can often find itself in opposition to natural tendencies or inclinations.

---

3 Richard Dawkins, *The Selfish Gene*, London: Granada Publishing, 1978, p. 205.

4 Tennyson, *In Memoriam*.

5 T. H. Huxley, *Evolution and Ethics*, London: Pilot Press, 1949.

An evolutionary account of human behaviour shows how this can be so – because what proved advantageous in the far past may be fatal now.

The Evolutionary World-view

When Aquinas wrote, he did not have an evolutionary world-view. He was assuming an Aristotelian world-view, according to which all things have final causes, end-states towards which they strive by an inherent purposiveness. Modern science ejects all such final causes from the physical world, or at least refuses to consider them. Physicists speak of initial states and laws governing physical change. But they do not speak of states for the sake of which physical entities exist, and towards which they strive.

A natural inclination, for Aristotle, is the movement of a thing towards its final cause. That final cause is also usually the formal cause, the true definition of a thing. The idea is that things move towards the proper actualization of their essential natures. But for modern physics, there are no essential natures, and no purposive movement towards them. It is in biology that relics of Aristotelian final and formal causality may still be found. We can think of an acorn as tending towards its final cause, an oak tree. We can think of a fertilized egg as tending towards the goal of producing a new animal. Taking food has the purpose of maintaining a body in existence.

But Darwinian accounts of evolution, even more than modern physics, place a large question mark against such teleological pictures of biological nature. Suppose we ask the question, 'Is there a purpose towards which the evolutionary process moves?' Among biologists this is a highly disputed issue. Biologists like Stephen J. Gould held that human life is not the purpose of evolution.[6]

---

6 Stephen J. Gould, *Wonderful Life*, London: Penguin, 1989.

Humans are just what happened not to be exterminated by early environments – and they may exterminate themselves very soon, leaving ants or beetles to inherit the earth. Others, however, like Simon Conway Morris, argue that even from a purely physical point of view a tendency can be seen in evolution, towards the development of conscious and intelligent life.[7]

Anyone who believes in a creator God is almost bound to believe that God created the universe for a purpose, and that therefore the evolutionary process must be purposive in some sense, must tend towards the goal God has set for it. For Christians and other believers in a creator God, that goal at least partly consists in the existence of finite beings capable of a conscious loving relationship with one another and with the creator. The goal is the existence of persons capable of conscious relationship with God, and the physical processes of evolution must be consistent with that.

Despite the fact that evolution is widely seen by biologists as undirected and largely random, it would be widely agreed that the process at least looks as though it leads to the emergence of more complex organisms and to intelligent life. It looks goal-directed, and so the Christian is on strong ground in thinking that it is goal-directed. Nevertheless virtually all biologists agree that the process of evolution, even if it is goal-directed in general, is one that operates largely by random mutation and natural selection.

Mutations are random in that not all of them are conducive to improvements in the efficiency or well-being of organisms. Indeed the majority of mutations are harmful to organisms, leading to their extinction, and many more mutations have no tendency to organic 'improvement'. Only a very few mutations are beneficial, though that tiny minority that do give a survival-advantage naturally tend to replicate and flourish exponentially. In such a process, one can speak of a 'natural tendency' only with some care. The process as a whole

---

7 Simon Conway Morris, *Life's Solution*, Cambridge: Cambridge University Press, 2003.

may have a tendency to produce intelligent life, but in its particular details the tendency looks more like a trial-and-error process in which there are vastly many more errors than successes. Even when there are beneficial mutations, they need to be selected by the environment. Such 'natural' selection is actually a process of killing off the less well adapted rather than a matter of positive and prudential encouragement. God may have set up the process for a good end, but it is hard to think that the extermination of species, a natural and probably inevitable part of the evolutionary process, is something positively willed as good in itself, by God. Believers in God must think extinction of species is an inevitable consequence of the evolutionary process, and it is that process as a whole that is positively willed by God. So the evolutionary process, as seen by most biologists, causes vast amounts of harm, and seems wasteful and ruthless. Most individual organisms are doomed to extinction; in fact all are doomed to die.

Death is not the result of some primordial human sin. It was an essential feature of organic existence millions of years before humans came into existence. We might well say that all organisms have a natural tendency to die. Death, as seen by evolutionary biologists, is certainly natural, and not any sort of corruption of organic existence. Anyone who accepts these evolutionary beliefs – and that is most competent evolutionary biologists – must say that, if there is purpose in the process, it is hardly a purpose that should not be improved if one had the ability and wisdom to do so.

The biological world, as seen by evolutionary biologists, is most certainly not in order as it is, to be respectfully left alone as the ordinance of the creator. To put it bluntly, nature does not always act for the best. It naturally produces a majority of harmful mutations. So there seems little reason to say that there is any sort of moral obligation to leave natural processes alone. If one can identify some good or beneficial effects of mutation, they should be chosen and protected, even if that means interfering with natural processes of mutation and selection. For the natural processes produce much harm, which rational interference might be able to prevent. They work by trial and error, and by ruthless methods of extinction (like the extinction event that wiped out the dinosaurs 65 million years ago, which enabled humans to evolve). Of course, this is just why Charles Darwin came to doubt the kindly providence (though not the existence) of God.

Natural processes do not seem to be perfectly designed in detail by a benevolent intelligence. I can see why many Christians find Darwinian evolution a threat to faith. Now a Darwinian account of evolution, in terms of random mutation and natural selection, may be misguided in some way. But suppose we accept it, as the best established theory there is for explaining the development of intelligent life, what are the consequences for Christian belief? A Christian has to believe that God is a benevolent intelligence who designs and creates the cosmos. It seems to follow that the general process of evolution must be intelligently, efficiently ordered to produce its specific effects. It must be goal-directed and benevolent in intention. We could defend such a belief if the general structure of physical laws which make this cosmos possible entails that the evolutionary process must function in the way it does, by mutation and cumulative selection of adaptive mutations. The process is based on supremely elegant laws, and perhaps it can be guaranteed to produce intelligent life, which can share in the life of supreme goodness.

In addition, we need to note the fact that the pessimistic view of nature as 'red in tooth and claw' is not universally shared by biologists. Tennyson himself, from whom that famous quotation comes, ends his poem *In Memoriam* by referring to 'One God, one law, one element, And one far-off divine event, To which the whole creation moves.' There are balancing views of evolution, like those of Frans de Waal, Erik Parens, and Steven Rose, that see the neo-Darwinian stress on competition, selfishness and survival as one-sided. Brian Goodwin, Professor of Biology at the Open University, UK, writes, 'We are every bit as co-operative as we are competitive; as altruistic as we are selfish; as creative and playful as we are destructive and repetitive. And we are ... agents of creative evolutionary emergence, a property we share with all other species.'[8] It is possible to see the evolutionary process as one of creative emergence and dynamic interrelationship, rather than as one of ruthless competition for mere replication. There is competition and destruction. But there is also what seems to many biologists to be a holistic emergent and self-organizing propensity to complexity, order and consciousness. If that is so, there may be positive value in the evolutionary process, as one that makes possible a partly self-shaping creative advance towards intelligent consciousness.

In some such way, belief in evolution as the vehicle of divine creation can be defended. But not every part of the natural process will be desirable. Although the process as a whole is designed to effect a good end, many of its particular parts cause great harm. In that case, it would seem irresponsible to think that all natural processes should be left as they are, even if we become able to reduce the number of harmful mutations, or to mitigate some of the more ruthless aspects of the struggle for existence.

In the practice of medicine, we have begun to do this. Humans sometimes keep the less healthy members of the species alive, often at great expense. And there is hope of eliminating some of the most harmful genetic mutations (like that for cystic fibrosis), by bio-chemical manipulation of genes. Clearly, we do not believe that natural processes are good in themselves. They are good only when they issue in rationally desirable outcomes. What is intended by God may be discernible in the facts of human behaviour. If God has a purpose in evolution, we should be able to discern, at least in a general way, what that purpose is by seeing what valued states natural processes tend to produce.

Looking at human nature from an evolutionary point of view, it is plausible to say that the purpose of the process is the production of

---

8 Brian Goodwin, *How the Leopard Changed its Spots*, London: Weidenfeld & Nicolson, 1994, p. xiv.

conscious, intelligent, morally responsible and spiritually aware forms of life. It follows that Christian moral obligation will be to help in realizing that purpose, and to refrain from frustrating it. That is a sort of 'natural law' morality – seeing what the distinctive nature of human life is, seeing how that can be a divinely ordained purpose, and consequently resolving to act in accordance with the purpose of the natural process, to act in accordance with nature.

However, saying this in a Darwinian context is very different from saying it in an Aristotelian context. An Aristotelian view sees human nature as a matter of the striving of all material beings to realize their proper Form or nature. If we can identify this Form, we will know what a human being 'ought' to be, what it properly, in its most mature form, is. And if we see how organisms tend to behave, we will see what the proper end of their activity is. All things naturally tend to realize their proper natures.

There is a sense in which Christians are bound to be sympathetic to this idea. God must have an idea of what God wants humans to be. If we can identify that idea, we will know how humans should act to realize it. For Christians, human existence is a striving to realize an ideal that exists in the mind of God. In that sense, it is true that we should strive to realize our proper natures. We should seek to become what God wants us to be, to conform to the image of humanity in the mind of God.

But from an evolutionary view, the process by which humans come to exist is not one in which each thing is striving to become what it ought to be. It is one in which there is a huge amount of trial and error, and the elimination of many organisms because of their lack of adaptation with the environment. The process does seem to be well constructed to produce intelligent life forms sooner or later. But it is not one all of whose details command our moral respect, or demand our moral submission to all its natural tendencies or inclinations.

On an Aristotelian view, it makes sense to say that we should act in accordance with nature, in the sense that our natural inclinations will show us what we ought to be (they are our proper strivings leading towards our essential nature). But for an evolutionary view, acting in accordance with nature will have to be interpreted as helping to realize the general purpose of the evolutionary process as a whole. Not all our natural inclinations will show us what that is, for some natural inclinations will be remnants of ancient behavioural tendencies that may now be harmful, and others will simply have failed to exterminate us so far, since they have not been eliminated by natural selection, though they have no positive function. Our natural inclinations will no longer show us what we ought to be or do. Rather, we will have to discriminate between genetically programmed tendencies that are conducive to the general purpose of enabling intelligent life to flourish, and others that are inefficient in doing so, or that even frustrate the possibility of doing so.

Reflection on distinctive human capacities is a guide to what the divine purpose in evolution may be. But having decided on that, we then have to judge genetically programmed tendencies on their success in helping to achieve such a purpose. Many of the ways in which some organisms act will ensure their extinction (most species become extinct). And even if they thrive, some organisms are intrinsically harmful to other organisms (viruses are generally harmful to organic bodies, for example). This blocks any move from seeing how things naturally behave to saying that it is good that they behave in that way. It looks as if we have to identify intrinsically good states first, and then ask whether natural processes are apt to achieve them. It is unsatisfactory to look at how things naturally behave in order to see what states are good.

Aquinas confines his remarks about natural law to very general principles. When he considers natural inclinations, he outlines three main types of natural inclination – one shared with all substances, namely, the appetite to self-preservation. The second is what humans share with animals – sexual intercourse and the bringing up of the young. The third is inclinations of beings of a rational nature – including knowledge of God and what relates to living in society (friendship and so on). Natural law covers 'everything to which man is set by his very nature'.[9] In an evolutionary world-view, we do not have to reject this principle. Human nature is purposively intended by God, and the inclinations Aquinas picks out – to survive, procreate, know and appreciate beauty and truth, and share friendship and love with others – are inclinations that seem necessary to realizing the divine purpose.

The belief that it is objectively wrong to frustrate these natural inclinations is an important safeguard against the view that human rights are simply conventions of governments or societies. Whatever the positive laws of particular countries may be, it is morally wrong to frustrate the ability of any human being to survive, found a family, and grow in knowledge and freedom. Acts hostile to human life, and acts that violate the integrity and dignity of the human person – like torture, enslavement and enforced prostitution – are morally wrong in themselves, and not just because some group of humans says so.

The doctrine of natural law is a vital foundation of belief in fundamental human rights. Natural law can, at least in its general outlines, be known by reason, and it is founded on the eternal will and purpose of God for human lives. But we have to say, more clearly than Aquinas did, that nature itself has no purposes, and not all her tendencies are good. It is God, not nature, who has purposes, though they are to be worked out in and through nature. They can indeed be discerned by reflection on nature, but only by discriminating what tends to the flourishing of personal life from what tends to frustrate such flourishing. An inspection of natural processes themselves will not enable such a discrimination to be made. It follows that it is not as such always wrong to frustrate some alleged 'purpose of nature'. It might be morally right to frustrate it if it diminishes a truly human good.

---

9 Aquinas, *Summa Theologiae*, 1a 2ae question 94, article 3.

It seems as if, from the perspective of modern biology, we can no longer speak of an obligation not to frustrate the purposes of nature. If it is not harmful to organisms, genetic engineering, whether by the use of drugs or the manipulation of genetic material, can even be morally obligatory. Major heritable diseases could be eliminated and human health much improved by genetic engineering, and the main moral criterion will be whether such engineering is conducive to the human flourishing of the individual (or the potential individual) concerned.

A Theology of Nature

There is something wrong, however, with the view that physical processes of nature are only of value in an instrumental sense, which implies that they have no value in themselves. Nature is created by God, and personal beings, however important they may be, have only existed for a minute fraction of the time during which the universe has existed. Nature forms the environment within which persons exist, and is the proper object of contemplation and delight, for humans as surely for God.

Just as it dishonours other persons to treat them merely as objects to be used, manipulated or cast aside, so it dishonours nature to treat it merely as an object to be used, manipulated or destroyed. God delights in the beauty of the natural world. In the millions of years before humans existed, the world was appreciated and valued by God for the good things it contains. When humans come to exist, they can enter into this appreciation and valuing. But humans do not give nature its value. They come to share in a valuing which has existed as long as God has existed.

For believers in God, nature is also a sacrament, in the wide sense of a physical expression of a spiritual presence. In the beauty of mountains and forests, desert and sea, there exists a physical expression of one part of the infinite being of God. As Schleiermacher put it, to see the infinite in the finite is true piety,[10] and nature is the medium through which infinity can be manifested in some of its myriad forms. The proper human attitude to nature should therefore be one of reverence and appreciation, as it is valued not only because God values it and takes delight in it, but also because it can mediate and express the beauty and wisdom of God.

This compels us to say that nature does not just exist instrumentally, as a means for bringing persons into existence. It has an intrinsic value of its own, as a sacrament of the divine presence, as an object of contemplation and delight, and as the widest boundary of the personal self, helping to constitute personhood and make personhood what it is, not only to support it as some sort of alien entity. This is the central moral point made by those who promote what is now known as 'deep ecology', the view that nature has value in its own right. The term was first used by the environmental philosopher Arne Naess, in an attempt to counter the widespread view that nature only has instrumental value.

Warwick Fox says: 'The ecological self of a person is that with which this person identifies.'[11] The hopeless egoist identifies with just one body and complex of feelings and thoughts. The tribalist identifies with a particular social group – in England, it might be Manchester United soccer club – which gives meaning and identity. Humanists embrace the whole human race in the range of their moral concern. But it is possible to go further, to include animals, then plants, and finally, to experience 'a commonality with all that is'. This is the widest possible range of moral concern. To approach it requires a revolution in perception.

We have tended, Fox says, to see humans – and male humans especially – as autonomous rational beings who stand over against

---

10 F. W. Schleiermacher, *On Religion: Speeches to its Cultured Despisers*, Second speech, final sentence, tr. Richard Crouter, Cambridge: Cambridge University Press, 1988, p. 140

11 Warwick Fox, 'Transpersonal ecology and the varieties of identification', in Roger Gottlieb (ed.), *This Sacred Earth: Religion, Nature, and Environment*, London: Routledge, 1996, p. 436.

nature, for whose sake nature exists, who have dominion over nature, and use nature as a means to their own self-chosen purposes. It requires an inversion of thought to see humans as just one species among millions of others which have value, no more or less than other species and individuals do, as parts of nature. 'We and all other entities are aspects of a single unfolding reality.' Bron Taylor spells it out thus: 'Evolution means that there is no basis for seeing humans as more advanced or valuable than any other species . . . evolution has no telos.'[12]

For deep ecologists, 'the earth is primary and humans are derivative'.[13] Humans are one part of a complex and interconnected ecological system in which all species ought to be able to fulfil their evolutionary destinies. They have a right to survive and flourish. For such a vision, the idea of human stewardship is flawed. Catholic philosopher John Haught writes: 'Stewardship . . . is still too managerial a concept to support the kind of ecological ethic we need today.'[14] And Ruth Page says of the word 'dominion', 'I judge the word to be so dangerous that it is to be departed from in any contemporary doctrine of creation.'[15] Humans may have responsibility to help the parts of nature to fulfil their potential as harmoniously as possible, but 'mastery' is too likely to lead to lack of responsibility, lack of feeling, respect and care for the things of nature.

I think this call to an inversion of viewpoint, to a turning from anthropocentricity to a more cosmic moral vision is enlightening and timely. But there are some questions to be raised. One main question concerns the sacredness of nature. Is the cosmos, or are the elements of the natural world, sacred? That is to say, are they worthy of reverence and worship? The Nature who speaks in Tennyson's *In*

---

12 Bron Taylor, 'Earth First: from primal spirituality to ecological resistance', in Gottlieb, *Sacred Earth*, p. 547.

13 Thomas Berry, 'Into the Future', in Gottlieb, *Sacred Earth*, p. 411.

14 John Haught, 'Christianity and Ecology', in Gottlieb, *Sacred Earth*, p. 277.

15 Ruth Page, *God and the Web of Creation*, London: SCM Press, 1966, p. 130.

Memoriam, 'red in tooth and claw',[16] bloody, indifferent, amoral and blind, is rather different from Gaia, the Goddess Earth who gives birth to her children, nourishes them, and binds them together in interconnected and beneficent harmony. The evolutionary process which exterminates millions of species and has no purpose seems quite different from an evolutionary process which gives to all beings the right to survive and flourish.

Allan Brockway says: 'Human beings transgress their divine authority when they destroy or fundamentally alter the rocks, the trees, the air, the water, the soil, the animals – just as they do when they murder other human beings.'[17] But what if there is no divine authority? Just the blind processes of chance and necessity? What then is the basis of a moral code?

It is hard to see that a process as morally ambiguous as nature can be intrinsically worthwhile. The mother goddess, where she is worshipped, after all, is not wholly benign. In Indian traditions, Durga wears a necklace of human skulls and wades in blood. This image is not stressed by deep ecologists, who tend to write rather sentimentally, to James Lovelock's alarm, of Gaia as our Mother. It is, of course, quite possible to see the divine as ruthlessly destructive as well as creatively beneficent. One can worship out of fear as well as out of gratitude. But this does introduce a moral ambiguity into the idea of the divine which is alien to Christian reflection. It is not at all clear that, accepting such ambiguity, one is obliged, as deep ecologists sometimes suggest, to grant to all beings in nature the right to survive and flourish.

Nature and the Resurrection

There is, I think, good reason to distance a creator God from nature, if we are to call God of supreme value, worthy of worship. Those

---

16 Tennyson, *In Memoriam*, stanza 56.

17 Allan R. Brockway, 'A Theology of the Natural World', *Engage/Social Action* 23 (July 1973).

who believe in God will think that there are many good things in nature, and that perhaps its cruelties, or many of them at least, are somehow necessary consequences or concomitants of the goods it produces. But though nature may in many ways reflect and express the beauty and wisdom of God, it is not itself supremely perfect by any means. It is at best an ambiguous sacrament of the divine presence.

But can nature become perfect? The doctrine of the resurrection of the body entails that there is a resurrection of the physical environment of which bodies are part. Those who believe in resurrection, knowing that every atom in our bodies has existed and will exist again in countless forms of physical reality, seem committed to believing that all physical reality will be resurrected in some way.

In the case of creatures who live and die, resurrection is often taken to mean a bringing back to conscious life. In the case of the physical environment, it will mean creating a form of existence free from frustration, decay, destruction and pain. Can we begin to imagine that? Perhaps it is not too hard to imagine God as knowing, in the closest possible way, every element of physical reality. Such knowledge will presumably be held in the divine mind without loss for ever. Wherever there are disvalues in nature, those will be sublated in God. That is to say, evil will be mitigated in its immediacy, transformed by the context of goodness within which it exists, and given meaning within the pattern of striving and overcoming of which it has been part. In the final harmony of God's awareness, the natural world might at last become fully the proper object of contemplation, admiration, awe and gratitude, a completed narrative of victory won through commitment, risk, renunciation and striving, of which the crucified and risen Lord is both archetype and fulfilment.

We might think of such a reconciliation and harmony of all things as existing in the divine mind, which redeems time by sublating evil and transfiguring the temporal into the eternity of the divine life. Yet that pictures God as a solitary contemplator of the completed history of the cosmos. The Christian vision of resurrection goes further. It promises conscious life to those who die in this cosmos, an embodied, if transfigured, life. So the objects of the divine consciousness do not remain as private objects of God's contemplation. They must take objective form, becoming the environment within which humans can be resurrected. God's thinking of a redeemed universe becomes God's creating of such a universe, visible and tangible in its own way by countless creatures. The redeemed world is not just God's private mental theatre. It is a public world of beauty and wisdom, in which creatures find that proper fulfilment which was so ambiguously expressed in this universe, and in which they share with God that ceaseless creativity and co-operation which are the chief marks of divine perfection. If any such harmony is possible, it will be beyond the thermodynamic laws of the cosmos in which we now exist. It will be a cosmos reconciled and at peace, in which no life forms have to kill to live, and all of nature will be an unambiguous sacrament of the divine life. The resurrection world will be very different from this: not a simple continuation, but a wholly new creation. But will all forms of beauty be there, from mountains to roses, from frogs to chimpanzees, all forming an environment which delights God and all conscious beings, and which is at last entirely good without flaw? I think that is what resurrection implies.

Resurrection is the resurrection, the apotheosis, of the cosmos, not just of human beings. This does not decrease the importance of the present. It matters enormously, it is of eternal significance, what we now do in and to our world. If we can help new forms of beauty to exist, they will exist in God and in the resurrection world that God creates for ever. If we destroy beauty, then there are forms which could have been, but now will never be. There will be absences where there could have been presences, and what we disfigure now will change what will be hereafter. So hope for resurrection is of immense ethical relevance to what we do now.

Nature and Christian Belief

I have suggested that a Christian view has some natural affinity with the recent development of deep ecology, and that the existence of God provides a rationale for reverence of nature as God's creation. But there is sometimes hostility between those who declare allegiance to deep ecology and traditional Christians. This hostility has many roots. Some of them are brought out in one of the formative papers in the modern discussion of the theology of nature, by the medieval historian Lynn White. In 1967, he wrote that 'Christianity bears a huge burden of guilt' for the exploitation and destruction of the natural world, which has now gone so far that some even speak of the 'end of nature'. He points out that in some traditional Christian theology, 'no item in the physical creation had any purpose save to serve man's purposes'.[18] As Thomas Aquinas put it, 'The whole of material nature exists for man, inasmuch as he is a rational animal.'[19] Again, 'we believe all corporeal things to have been made for man's sake'. White comments, 'Christianity is the most anthropocentric religion the world has seen.'[20] If only human beings have immortal souls, and if God is concerned only for the redemption of humans, then the rest of nature has only instrumental value.

To make it worse, Genesis 1.28 states that humans are to subdue and have dominion over the earth. The Hebrew term for subdue is *kabash*, and the term for dominion is *radah*. Those Hebrew words have the connotation of conquest, domination, even enslavement. And the evidence is, White claims, that this is how they have been interpreted for much of Christian history. Nature, including environment, plants, and animals, can be regarded as mere lumps of

---

18 Lynn White, 'The Historic Roots of Our Ecologic Crisis', in Gottlieb, *Sacred Earth*, p. 189.

19 Cited in H. Paul Santmire, *The Travail of Nature: The Ambiguous Ecological Promise of Christian Theology*, Philadelphia: Fortress Press, 1985, p. 91.

20 White, 'Historic Roots', p. 189.

matter, to be used purely for human enjoyment. The denial of spirits in trees and rivers, which is characteristic of Christian faith, helped to make it possible to treat nature as an object to be used, rather than as an object of reverence and intrinsic value. These factors have, White argues, led to the unfettered despoliation of the natural world, and the alienation of human beings from their natural environment. Certainly, if one thinks that animals and natural objects have value which is to be respected, the historical record of Christianity is not good. So White argues that 'We shall continue to have a worsening ecologic crisis until we reject the Christian axiom that nature has no reason for existence save to serve man.'[21]

White is himself a Christian, and his article is a confession of past inadequacies and a call to a renewed Christian vision of nature as a creation beloved of God. But it has been taken by many as an attack on Christianity, as the anthropocentric, dominating desacralizer of nature. Those who look for some spiritual vision which does not suffer from these disorders often look elsewhere, to some form of animism or goddess worship, or to what are characterized in a vague way as 'Eastern religions'. The earth can be seen as our Mother, Gaia, generating and sustaining life, or nature can be seen as a realm of spirits with rights or interests: so Bron Taylor writes, 'Evolution means that there is no basis for seeing humans as more advanced than any other species.'[22] Even Process philosophy can take an animistic tone at times; all beings have 'a potential for richness of experience', which should be respected, John Cobb writes.[23] It is not surprising that traditional Christians feel some alarm at the apparent devaluation of personhood, the attribution of quasi-personal characteristics and rights to natural processes which are normally thought to be non-sentient, and the identification of the divine with the morally ambiguous processes of evolution.

---

20 White, 'Historic Roots', p. 193.

21 Gottlieb, *Sacred Earth*, p. 547.

23 John Cobb Jr. and Charles Birch, *The Liberation of Life*, Cambridge: Cambridge University Press, 1981, p. 170.

The frequent appeal to Eastern religions as superior sources of moral insight also does not generally commend itself to traditional Christians. Some writers have held that the 'Eastern' religions teach a greater unity with nature than the Abrahamic faiths, and Christianity in particular. 'Asian faiths', writes Roderick Nash, 'never abandoned a sense of the unity of nature and subscribed to an ethical philosophy that did not begin and end with people.'[24] This, it must be said, is a very selective presentation of Asian faiths. One of the most important Hindu religious systems is that of Sankhya, which views the world as consisting of *purusa*, spirit, and *prakriti*, matter. Matter may not be evil, but it deludes spirit into thinking that spirit is material. The way of release from suffering is to abandon all desires which attach one to the material, and to realize one's true nature as pure spirit. This is hardly a matter of seeing oneself as part of an organic whole.

In a similar way, in most Buddhist systems attachment to the material world inevitably brings suffering in its train, and one must renounce desire in order to attain nirvana, complete transcendence of nature. Moreover, in almost all Buddhist schools being human is the only form of embodiment that gives the possibility of enlightenment, so that humans do have an immensely privileged position over other life forms (and men often have greater privileges than women). It is just false that Asian faiths as such have a sense of the unity of nature which is non-anthropocentric.

There is much to be learned from many Asian religious traditions. We could well learn from Buddhism a sense of universal compassion for all sentient beings which has not been a marked feature of Christianity. We could learn a love of the rhythms and balance of nature from some aspects of Chinese Taoist thought. But just as Christian traditions are complex, so are Indian and Chinese traditions. It would be quite wrong to say, either that Hindus and Buddhists see nature as something to be escaped from, or that they see human lives as in organic unity with the natural world. The truth

---

24 'The Greening of Religion', in Gottlieb, *Sacred Earth*, p. 198.

is that both these strands of thought exist in Asian traditions, as they do in the Christian.

If one is going to make a broad generalization, it might be that the Indian traditions rarely conceive of nature as having a positive purpose, or as having some sort of lasting destiny (though some do). Insofar as Christians speak of resurrection, and of a new heaven and earth, they stress the materiality of the human person – and therefore the essential importance of its embeddedness in nature – more than most Indian traditions do. So those who find Eastern faiths intrinsically superior to the Christian in this respect simply have not presented the evidence adequately. Each tradition has much to repent of, and something to offer, in the search for a more adequate understanding of and ethical relation to nature.

It is because nature is red in tooth and claw, but also beautiful and awe-inspiring in its manifold striving for greater life, that there is an important place for a distinctive Christian theology of nature. In that theology, nature itself will not be divine. Nor will it be cruel or indifferent. It will be a process with an innate propensity towards developing beings of consciousness and responsible action, who can share in the divine creative power to shape the world to infinite forms of beauty, and share in the divine comprehension of all created things. In this process conscious responsible agents will have a special role. It will sometimes be the role of a conqueror, when it is the destructive power of earthquakes, tornadoes, of animals of prey and viruses that must be conquered. It will more often be the role of steward, guarding and creating beauty, and of enjoyer, delighting in that beauty. It will also be the role of worshipper, revering not nature in itself, but God, the wise though often unfathomable intelligence that is known in and through nature and that expresses the divine nature in the refracted and multitudinous forms of the cosmos, but always remains beyond the ambiguities and imperfections of nature.

There is a proper anthropocentricity in Christian thinking about nature, but it is one of responsibility, not of dominance. Persons – and humans are the most fully developed persons on this planet –

have the responsibility of creating, reverencing and shaping nature. Because of their responsible freedom (not because of their species-membership only), they have a moral dignity which seems unique to them. There is a proper sense of dominion. But, as Genesis 2.15 suggests, humans are to tend or take care of the earth, not destroy or neglect it. Dominion is the delegated care of the world God creates with love, and for that stewardship all humans will be called to account. There is a sacredness in nature, but it lies in its capacity to express in many finite forms transcendent divine perfection, and that capacity can be fully realized only when nature is liberated from its suffering and destructiveness, in a renewed creation.

The Christian vision of nature is that, though all things come to destruction, and though nature appears at times to be indifferent to the fate of the lives it generates, it can nevertheless reasonably be affirmed that, as Tennyson puts it, love is creation's final law. For nature can be in many of its aspects a sacrament of that perfect goodness which is God. In it we find the challenge to eliminate suffering and pain, and shape it to forms of beauty and happiness, caring for all living things, so far as is possible, with compassion and delight. And within it there is the hope and promise of ultimate fulfilment, when the whole cosmos will be transfigured by God, and filled with the glory, the beauty, creative power and infinite wisdom of God, as the waters cover the sea. Then nature will be, as it is not yet, the unambiguous sacrament of God, to be properly reverenced and delighted in as a self-expression of the divine life, and the final fulfilment of the divine purpose in creation.

Trans-humans and the Soul

There is thus in the Christian tradition, and in Judaism and Islam too, in slightly different ways, the thought that the present state of the natural world is not its final state. There is even the thought that, for whatever reason, the present state has been corrupted in some way. So there is little reason to be afraid of the proposal, which only became a realistic one with the growth of technology since the sixteenth century, that nature as it is can and should be improved by human action.

More hesitation may be felt about proposals to improve on humanity, and maybe to breed a species of super-humans. From a traditional Christian point of view, are humans not made in the image of God, and so should they not be preserved as they are? There may be much debate about what the image of God actually is. Many early Christian theologians interpreted it to mean that humans have knowledge and freedom and creative power, as God does. But in that case it would seem that the more knowledge and power a finite creature had, the more it would reflect the divine image. It is reasonable to think that it is God's will that we should grow in knowledge, intellectual ability and moral freedom. If we can find genes that will increase such abilities, taking them beyond present human capacities, that would then seem to be in accordance with God's will. After all, many Christians think that Jesus had super-human miraculous knowledge and powers, but he was still truly human. So there does not seem to be a religious barrier to improving the human species in its intellectual and moral capacities, if we can.

Christians have also traditionally believed in the existence of super-human species like angels, so there seems to be no bar in principle to creating super-human species, perhaps like some form of artificial intelligence, if the time comes when we can do so. In such a situation, we would have to be careful to accord such beings the same sorts of rights that morally free human beings have. But I see no reason why humans should think of themselves as the highest form of created personal life. God loves all creatures, and the human situation may be a relatively humble one in the cosmic scheme of things. That would not lessen human responsibility at all, and might even give it a greater importance in the process of cosmic evolution. Humans may be able to become part-directors of their own future evolution beyond humanity.

One traditional argument against this is that the physical bodies we actually have are an integral part of what we are, and they should not be treated as mere instruments, that we can change or discard just as we wish. God has created us as the body-soul unities that we are, and we are not morally free to change our bodies or our characters by artificial manipulation. Such an objection is based on the view, which is certainly a traditional Christian one, that human bodies must be seen as parts of one integral and unitary personal reality, and are not disposable bits of mechanism. Despite some popular beliefs to the contrary, the traditional Christian view of human persons is that they are physical bodies, animals, that possess emergent properties of consciousness and volition. To speak of a 'soul' is to speak of the capacities of a type of physical body, capacities of a type of animal capable of abstract thought and responsible action. Souls cannot properly exist without bodies – a view Aquinas espoused.[25]

The complication here is that the soul is often also spoken of by Aquinas as though it were a non-physical agent of thought, action, sensation and perception. Some form of embodiment may be essential to it, in order to provide information, and the possibility of communication and action. But perhaps the same soul could be embodied in different forms. Anyone who believes in reincarnation must believe this.

Catholic Christians, who do not share belief in reincarnation, do nevertheless seem to be committed to the existence of souls, both in purgatory and in heaven, that have consciousness and experience, but do not have ordinary physical bodies. Moreover, whatever the resurrection body is, it is certainly not temporally or physically continuous with this physical body, and it may be significantly different in some respects (it will not be corruptible, and will not have exactly the same physical properties).[26] Aquinas said that disembodied souls

---

25 Aquinas, *Summa Theologiae*, 1a, question 76.
26 1 Corinthians 15.

may exist 'improperly and unnaturally', by the grace of God, and will not fully be persons again until the resurrection.[27] But it is obvious that a resurrected body will not be constituted of the same physical stuff as present bodies (it is said to be spiritual, not physical). The present physical universe will come to an end, and there will be 'a new heaven and earth'. What that means is that the physical stuff of this specific universe is not essential to the nature and continuous existence of persons, even if something analogous to this body must exist.

What is at stake in this discussion is whether human consciousness is an emergent property of a physical object – and so ceases to function or exist without that object. Or whether human consciousness, though it does originate within a physical body, and does require some form of embodiment for its full and proper functioning, is nevertheless dissociable from its original body, and is capable of existence in other forms. Is the soul adjectival to the body, or is this body just one form in which this soul may exist? Aquinas tries to straddle both sides of this divide by speaking of the soul as a 'subsistent form', something whose function it is to give a body specific capacities, but which is capable of existing, though not of functioning in its full and proper way, without that body.

It is this point that many biologists and psychologists have great difficulty accepting. Many of them can see intelligence as an emergent property of a physical organism. But they are resolutely opposed to any form of vitalism, of a view that the body is actually regulated in its physical organization and structure by a spiritual principle or agency, whether this is called a 'soul' or a 'form'. This may seem a rather recondite philosophical dispute, but actually it shows the importance of views of human nature to morality. Our view of what a person is may make a very important difference to the moral precepts we accept. If we insist on the primary importance of humans as body-soul unities, then the body should not be regarded

---

27 Aquinas, *Summa Theologiae*, 1a, question 76, article 1.

as simply 'raw material', something 'extrinsic to the person', that can be shaped or dealt with in any way one wishes. The unity of soul and body means that we must respect our bodily structure, since that is part of what we essentially are – 'body and soul are inseperable', and the body intrinsically has moral meaning.

We might contrast this view with some Hindu views that the body is just a garment that we put on or off. For Aquinas, the body is constitutive of what we are, and we would not be the same being without it, without the specific body we have. This is what is intended by the traditional Catholic view that each soul is fitted for a specific body. We might say that each soul is the unique soul of a unique body. From this two things have been said to follow. First, the finality of our bodily tendencies cannot be regarded as purely physical or pre-moral. Our bodily structure and inclinations are morally relevant, and relate directly to the fulfilment of the total human person, body and soul. Second, each person, as created in the image of God and ordered towards participation in the life of God, has intrinsic dignity and inviolability. It may therefore be thought that we are morally obliged not to perform any act that would change or modify our own unique body and character as it has been given to us in our creation.

However, I do not think this follows. Suppose we agree that persons are physical organisms with intellectual or spiritual capacities. These capacities are rooted in a non-physical entity, capable of non-physical existence, but the proper functioning of which is within the specific physical body which is part of its proper being, and which has always to some degree limited and shaped its operation. This is what the philosopher Charles Taliaferro calls 'integrative dualism',[28] and it seems to me to describe the traditional Catholic view rather well. What follows from this account?

Certainly, that human bodies are not mere adjuncts of persons.

---

28 Charles Taliaferro, *Consciousness and the Mind of God*, Cambridge: Cambridge University Press, 1994.

When they are functioning properly, they should express a personal life. Bodily acts are personal acts. Part of human flourishing is bodily flourishing, and that means due realization of the capacities and excellences of the body. The most basic moral principle this suggests is that of life and health. The body should not be abused. So while there is nothing wrong with eating for pleasure, the real purpose of eating is to produce a healthy body, and considerations of pleasure should be subordinate to that. The use of drugs and excessive wine or food is morally prohibited, and regular exercise is morally prescribed.

So what we have are principles enjoining acts that increase bodily and mental well-being and the highest use of bodily and mental capacities. They are not principles that can never be violated, but there must be very strong moral reasons for violating them. They are, in almost all cases, morally binding. However, it is fairly clear that it is the mental and spiritual capacities that are of primary importance. Often our bodies can frustrate our mental capacities, our abilities to do things, and in that case it is right to try to remove such frustrations, whether that is by the use of drugs or surgery. So if our bodies can be improved to enable our mental capacities to be better expressed, there seems every reason to do so.

From a religious point of view, the goal of human life is not simply to survive or to reproduce. It is to know and love God for ever. The possession of some body is important to us, because we are embodied souls. But our bodies exist primarily to express the capacities of the soul, and for those who believe in the resurrection of the body, those resurrected bodies will be more glorious and incorruptible by far than our present bodies.

In this way, I think a perception of the spiritual destiny of humanity suggests that the physical body does not have morally absolute status, and that the primary spiritual principle, besides the love of God, is the flourishing of personal life rather than the preservation of the present physical order, whatever it may be. The physical order may need to be ordered to the greater flourishing of sentient, intelligent and responsible life, before it fulfils what we might see to be its proper role.

A word of caution is needed. Religious believers are well aware of the power of sin, of hatred, greed and ignorance, of the will to power that corrupts every human ideal. In the search to create super-humans it would be easy to espouse forms of genetic selection that lead to the creation of an alleged 'master race'. In Nazi Germany Darwinian principles were misused by Haeckel and others to justify the elimination of the 'genetically unfit'. That is a nightmare scenario, and totally unacceptable morally. Any religious acceptance of genetic engineering would need to ensure that the 'unfit' were not eliminated, but cared for with compassion. And superiority would have to be defined in terms of superior love and compassion, not superior strength and power. The aim of acceptable biochemical manipulation of genes must be true human flourishing.

Christian revelation is of vital importance at precisely this point. For it helps to define what true human flourishing is. It demands that all bodily activities express love and concern for others, the strengthening of faithful and loyal friendship, and an ordering towards final fulfilment in the knowledge and love of God. But it does not demand (or, in its scriptural sources, even mention) a prohibition on frustrating 'the purposes of nature' as such. It does require that all physical activities are to be assessed and modified in the light of our spiritual orientations.

Thus our contemporary view of the cosmos as a vast evolutionary process suggests a revised view of natural law. There is a natural sense of right and wrong. It is deepened by the Christian revelation of a transcendent moral purpose in nature. But that must not be confused with alleged 'purposes' in the details of physical processes themselves. As humans come to take full responsibility for their future, they can begin to shape physical processes towards truly spiritual ends. The natural moral law, illumined by revelation, does not say: 'God has made this, do not interfere.' It rather says: 'God has given you responsibility for this; shape it wisely, always bearing in mind the goal of greater understanding, compassion and freedom.' Matters of morality remain matters for human decision. The Christian – and perhaps any acceptable religious – dimension is to make us the sort of persons who can make such decisions wisely, compassionately, and with love. Natural law, in its post-evolutionary form, points towards the future perfection of nature (though it does not guarantee any such thing at some point in our earthly future). It sets the direction in which humans might seek to shape nature. And thus it suggests a way in which one vocation of humans is to be responsible co-creators with God of a physical world that can more truly and fully express spiritual values.

4

Questions of Gender:
Christianity and Sexuality

If you say that you are going to write about religion and morality, many people immediately assume that you are going to write about sex. And I am. As a matter of fact I do not think that issues of sexuality and gender are the most important moral issues in the modern world. I would reserve that honour for questions of global justice (one theme of Chapter 6) and the proper conservation and use of the world's natural resources (one theme of Chapter 3). But questions of sex do immediately affect every human individual, and religions have had much to say about the morality of sexual practice.

It cannot be denied that a great deal of what has been said has been negative. For many religions in the Indian tradition, abstention from sexual practice is a condition of living an advanced spiritual life. In the Abrahamic faiths, that is not generally the case, but sexual practice is nevertheless strongly circumscribed by limiting it to slightly differing versions of exclusive marriage relationships, within which alone sexual relationships are permitted. In the modern world rapidly changing social conditions and the development of means of birth control have meant that for many people sexual relationships have become wholly a matter of personal choice, and ancient religious prohibitions seem to them to be strangely restrictive. Is there anything to be said any longer for the institution of exclusive life-long marriage, and for the prohibition of all sexual activity outside that institution? This is not just a dispute between religious and secular moral views. The opposition to homosexual partnerships, for instance, is based as strongly on deep-rooted human feelings of aversion as on any religious principles. Indeed, religious views, at their best, try to counteract the ingrained prejudice that encourages hatred of people with homosexual inclination and temperament.

Nevertheless, there are major religious traditions that wholly forbid extramarital sexual practice. Both traditional Islam and the Roman Catholic Church are best known for issuing such prohibitions. But to some extent within Islam and to a much greater and more public extent in modern Christianity there is deep moral division about the extent to which traditional moral views may be appropriately revised in the changed social and technological conditions of the modern world. In my discussion I shall focus on the Christian discussion. I shall seek to explore the roots of the traditional view that all sexual practice must be within lifelong marriage. Then I will examine the reasons that have been brought forward for challenging the traditional view. And I shall try to show what a revised morality of sexuality and gender might say, to provide a genuinely Christian view of human sexuality that is fully humane and liberating.

Sexuality and the Purposes of Nature

Traditional Christian views of sexuality have two main historical roots. One is the revealed Scripture, Old and New Testament, which seems to contain repeated condemnations of homosexual practice and of adultery – though it does not explicitly prohibit either polygamy or all extramarital sexual practices.

The other root is the tradition of natural law, which I discussed in the previous chapter. I suggested then that the traditional interpretation of natural law stands in need of revision, because of acceptance of an evolutionary world-view. In the traditional interpretation of natural law, inherited from Aristotle, the Stoics, and the thirteenth-century philosopher Thomas Aquinas, humans are said to have natural inclinations or tendencies. By examining these tendencies we can discern what the purposes of nature are, purposes that have been implanted in nature by God. It is always wrong to frustrate any of the purposes of nature, and this gives rise to a set of absolute prohibitions on practices that are contrary to the natural, God-created, order of things.

In the case of sexuality, the purpose of sexual practice is the procreation of offspring. Any sexual activity that does not leave open the possibility of procreation is thus unnatural and objectively disordered, for it is frustrating the purposes of nature. Such activities will include masturbation, any sexual acts that do not include a commitment to care for children who may result from such acts (i.e. marriage), and all homosexual physical acts. They are uses of the sexual organs that contradict their natural purposes, and so they are objectively disordered and unnatural. In my discussion of natural law, I pointed out that evolutionary biologists would generally give a much more morally neutral view of 'natural', or genetically ingrained, inclinations or tendencies. Some such tendencies, like hatred of foreigners, may be morally harmful. In sexual matters, natural human inclinations may actually need to be frustrated, if they frustrate moral purposes.

Most biologists would find it hard to discover moral purposes in nature itself. Where mutations are random, they can be improved. Where selection is by environment, we may adjust the environment to encourage the selection of desired characteristics. In the modern world, it is unwise just to leave nature as it is. We may often need to improve it. So the moral question is not what the purposes of nature are. Nature, for most biologists, has no purposes. God may indeed have moral purposes for nature. By reflection on distinctive human capacities, we may identify those purposes as including growth in consciousness, intelligence, compassion, responsibility and friendship. Those are the moral ideals to which the course of nature should be directed.

If that is so, morality should not be founded on preserving the present physical order, whatever it may happen to be. Morality should be founded on a discernment of what makes for the greater flourishing of personal life. Natural goods like those of creativity, contemplation and community, will enable us to identify those processes of nature that should not be frustrated, and those which should be frustrated or modified, because, however 'natural' they are, they frustrate the values of personal existence for the sake of which the natural cosmos exists.

Suppose, then, it is argued that, since sexual intercourse has the purpose of procreation, it is always wrong to frustrate that purpose. At once, most biologists would query whether it is true that the purpose of intercourse is procreation. When biologists consider sexual reproduction, they do not think that intercourse came into existence in order that there should be reproduction. For reproduction to take place, strands of DNA had to uncoil, replicate, and be embodied in a new cell capable of dividing. There are many ways in which this could happen, and intercourse is just one method of mixing DNA to form a new combination. We can now do it in a Petri dish in a medical laboratory. Sex happened to be quite efficient at forming new mutations some of which had a better chance of survival and replication. So sex is an efficient method of generating genetic variety and replication, resulting in the formation of new organisms.

If we say sex has the purpose of procreation, we do not mean that is what it was specifically designed for. We mean that it has worked well, up to now, in producing new animals. It is one method of producing new animals. It is natural, not in the sense that it has intrinsic moral worth as a method of reproduction, but in the sense that it is what has, by a process of trial and error, turned out to be reasonably successful in the struggle for reproductive survival. In short, sexual intercourse was not specifically designed by God to ensure procreation. It is just how procreation naturally takes place in humans, and we are not frustrating any divine designs if we decide to bring the process under rational and responsible control. If we make that decision, then moral questions about the creation of new human life are questions about how many and what sort of new humans should be generated, and in what conditions. When framed in that way, it becomes fairly clear that there is no obligation to produce as many new humans as possible, whatever they are like or whatever conditions they will be born into.

For anyone who believes in a creator, new life is a good, and it is a good thing for new persons to come into existence. But it is also good that new humans should have a fair chance of happiness, and a good and loving upbringing. It therefore seems reasonable to control the procreative process in order to produce children who will be loved and wanted. We might want to rule out a selfish motivation that ignores the good of procreation altogether, and also an irresponsible attitude that produces more children than we can feed or rear. But preventing the conception of unwanted children is not frustrating God's plan, at least not on a modern biological view of nature, for which successful conceptions and implantations are largely due to random processes or processes governed by general physical laws, the details of which are not specifically intended and determined by God.

A traditional view is that we should always leave open the possibility of procreation, but leave it to God when procreation is successful. That view was perhaps necessary in days when no effective control over procreation was possible. But now, from the biologists' viewpoint, it amounts to employing, in a rather haphazard way, one rather inefficient method of procreation, and leaving the outcome to chance. It would seem sensible to reduce the roles of both inefficiency and of chance in the process.

To some extent we could do this by utilizing the ovulatory cycle, but that is still markedly inefficient. It would be better to control ovulation more exactly by the use of chemicals. That would entail divorcing the sexual act from the natural possibility of procreation, for there would be many occasions when we knew conception could not occur. On such occasions – probably the vast majority in many human lives – the purpose of intercourse could not be procreation.

We would then be accepting the principle that sexual acts do not only have the 'purpose' of procreation. There are two other important aspects of human sexuality. Sexual acts give mutual pleasure, and they can express and reinforce the bonds of love between two people. These will be important, morally relevant considerations in considering what sexual acts are morally permissible.

Some people may regard sex as merely physical, a matter of producing pleasure, and as having no connection with other intellectual or even spiritual goods. But Christians see human bodies as parts of one integral and unitary personal reality, and physical activity cannot be simply disconnected from the involvement of the whole person. So if sexual activity is seen as impersonal or merely instrumental, this somehow misses the point that sexual activity is the activity of a person, whose nature is partly constituted by a body.

The use of the body is always expressive of the whole person. It can express self-centred, egotistical desires, or it can express concern for the health and well-being of others. When we interact with the bodies of others, we can use them as mere instruments to fulfil our own desires, or we can interact with them in ways that respect their unique personality and their ultimate calling to share in the life of God. The first set of uses in each case contradicts the good of the person, as a child of God and temple of the Holy Spirit. Personal selfishness and the treatment of others merely as means to our own purposes is wrong. This prohibits any sexual activity that demeans others or regards them as objects for our satisfaction. It prohibits any acts that undermine relationships of love, trust and fidelity between persons. And it prohibits acts that are purely self-centred.

Nevertheless, pleasure is not evil, and Christians have always supposed that it is right to enjoy the pleasures God gives, as long as they do not violate moral precepts. So can sexual activity not be enjoyed just for the pleasure it gives? It is here that we need to see sexual activity as an activity of the whole person, expressed in a specific bodily way. Sex is unitive in a special way. It is a physical uniting of persons, expressive of a mental and spiritual unity between them. Solitary sex cannot express that unitive aspect, and it is deficient in that respect. Its pleasure is essentially self-regarding. So it might seem to be prohibited, to be, as the Catholic Church teaches, 'objectively disordered'. Sex would be divorced from the possibility of procreation and from the expression of personal love and union. It would give a purely personal and individual pleasure. But does solitary sex actually make these goods more difficult or impossible in general?

Insofar as it does, I think we could say it is morally disordered. But it might not. Think of a person who will never live within a marriage, for whatever reason. Think of a person who is physically attracted to members of the same sex, and is genetically – that is, 'naturally' – inclined that way. For such persons, it is possible for sexual activity to produce mutual pleasure and express personal union. Homosexual or lesbian partnerships seem morally licit on these grounds, and rather more so than solitary masturbation, for at least they may express mutual love, and not solely be for personal gratification.

But masturbation, too, in a situation where procreation or union is not being frustrated, because there is no possibility of them (perhaps because of some physical disability, but not only that), does not seem to be always wrong. All personal pleasures are partly selfish. If that selfishness does not become a dominant drive, but is moderate and has no harmful effects on personality or human relationships, then, though it will hardly be a moral ideal, I would think there is no decisive moral objection to it.

The concept of objective disorder relies on a view of biological structures that subordinates considerations of the divine purpose for human life to considerations of how biological nature has come to be as it is through the course of evolution. If masturbation or same-sex union are disordered, it is not because they frustrate a 'purpose of nature'. There is no such purpose in nature itself. It is because they frustrate the purpose of God for human life. But if that purpose is of centring human life on love and care for others, then we may need to learn that committed, loyal, long-term, self-giving and mutual love between persons of the same sex seems, on these principles, to be something that could often be encouraged and defended.

Appeal to natural law is probably the major resource upon which Christian theologians rely in matters of sexual ethics. I have held that such an appeal is wholly reasonable, but that it needs to be revised in the light of evolutionary biology. We shall no longer be able to talk of frustrating the purposes of nature. Instead, we should speak of aiding or frustrating the purpose of God in creating the cosmos as a realm in which personal life emerges and develops, a purpose which is still in process, and which humans can help to implement in creative ways.

The Use of Scripture: 1. Christian Revisions of Torah

The other main source for Christian moral judgements in matters of gender and sexuality is Holy Scripture. Traditionally, specific texts condemning various forms of sexual practice have been accepted as binding rules for all time. But modern study of the Bible puts such uses of Scripture in question. For Christians there needs to be a much more sophisticated use of the Bible in ethical decision-making. I shall explore the way in which the ethical rules of the Bible have in practice been modified in many ways by Christian interpretation. I shall use this exploration to argue that further modifications are called for by changed modern social conditions. My conclusion will be that the biblical teaching on sexual morality is capable of a consistent, compelling and, for many people, rather surprising, interpretation.

The first and most obvious way in which Christians modify biblical moral rules rather drastically is to be found in the New Testament use of the Hebrew Bible, which becomes known as the 'Old Testament'. The astounding fact is that the New Testament abolishes Jewish religious law altogether for Christians. At the first

Church Council in Jerusalem (Acts 15.28), all the rules of the law were abolished except for eating blood or the flesh of animals that had been strangled – a remnant of the Jewish food laws. This is astounding because most of the apostles, including in particular James, the brother of Jesus, had supported keeping Torah, and Matthew records Jesus as saying that Torah should be kept (Matt. 5.17). The decision came only after 'much debate' (Acts 15.7), so it was plainly not a matter that had been conclusively settled by Jesus.

The Church took upon itself the authority to revoke Torah. Of course there was good reason for this, since Christians were now largely Gentile, and the decision was in effect that they did not have to become Jews before they could be Christians. Nevertheless, it was a decision of major importance. For Christians continued to accept the Hebrew Bible as their Scripture. Yet what Jews consider its major content, Torah, was henceforth regarded as the law for another religious group, not as such applicable to Christians. At a stroke, 613 commandments had been deprived of their binding authority for Christians.

Does this mean that all those commandments have no authority for Christians? In third-century Jewish thought, there was developed the idea of a Noahide covenant for Gentiles. This was said to consist of seven laws – the establishment of courts of justice, the prohibition of idolatry, blasphemy, sexual immorality, murder, theft and 'eating the limb from a living animal'. There has been much debate as to how to interpret these laws, but the Christian prohibition of eating blood could be an attempt to go back behind the Mosaic Law to God's covenant with Noah (recorded in Genesis 9.4).

It was not long before the prohibition on eating blood (kosher meat) was also abolished, showing that the process of revising religious law carried on beyond the New Testament. We have to conclude that Christians are neither bound by the laws of Torah nor by the written decisions of the Church recorded in the New Testament.

Calvin attempted to distinguish between the ritual parts of Torah and the moral parts, and retain the latter. There is no biblical precedent for doing that, and in any case Christians have revised or dropped some laws that seem undoubtedly to be moral. We do not approve of stoning our sons to death for drunkenness, or of letting the kin of murder victims kill their murderers, or of polygamy or concubinage, of Levirate marriage or of capital punishment for apostasy or witchcraft. We do not prohibit lending at interest, and we do not permit slavery. We may well not approve of capital punishment at all, and many Christians do not accept the Old Testament rules for divorce and remarriage.

Many of these laws had been dropped within Judaism by the time of Jesus, by general rabbinic consent. But the authority of the rabbis is not accepted by Christians, so that cannot be used as a reason for amending these biblical moral laws. Christians can regard the Church as having authority to revise or interpret biblical laws. But that means that the principle of revisability is accepted, under some conditions.

Some Christians (including Calvin) take the Ten Commandments as binding on Christians. There is no doubt that these commandments have a special importance, though significantly they omit the two most important commandments of the law, love of God and neighbour. But the first four commandments are not properly speaking moral. They prohibit worshipping other gods, making idols, misusing the name of God, and they enjoin keeping the Sabbath (not working, travelling, or lighting fires).

Jews, whose commandments these are, would probably say that Christians break at least two of them, for Christians have pictures of God (in the person of Jesus), and they do not keep the Sabbath rules properly. As Calvin saw (*Institutes*, Book 2, ch. 8), Christians can only make these laws their own by ignoring their literal sense, and giving them a spiritual sense. That is a major reinterpretation. So, again one must note here that Christians do not take all biblical laws in their literal sense, but often look for a rather remote spiritual sense (as when Calvin took the sabbath laws to denote a spiritual 'resting in God' – he opposed keeping one day of the week as a special religious festival, on the ground that we should be religious every day).

Calvin also decided to interpret each of the Ten Commandments as not only prohibiting some action, but also as positively enjoining the opposite action. Thus 'do not commit murder' enjoins 'save life', and 'do not steal' enjoins 'give freely to others'. This is a very agreeable interpretation, but it is pretty obviously not what the Bible says. What it seems to involve is the extension of the laws by applying the principle of neighbour-love as widely as possible. Given such freedom of interpretation, one may have a very free hand with many biblical rules.

The Use of Scripture: 2. Jesus' Moral Teaching

In addition to this fact of the rejection or spiritualization of biblical laws by the early Church and by many Christians, is another factor arising from the nature of Jesus' recorded moral teaching. I think it would be agreed that Jesus' moral teaching is found most crucially in Matthew's narrative of the Sermon on the Mount (Matt. 5—7). It is virtually impossible to interpret this teaching literally, or even to be quite sure exactly what it is recommending, in many cases. According to Matthew, Jesus says, 'You have heard that it was said, "An eye for an eye" (Matt. 5.38), But I say to you, do not resist an evildoer.' This is a crucial case for how we are to interpret the ethical teachings of the New Testament. Is Torah, given by God, being revoked by Jesus? It seems like it, yet the Sermon on the Mount begins with Jesus' statement, 'Do not think that I have come to abolish the law' (Matt. 5.17).

Perhaps, then, Jesus is keeping the law of retaliation as a legal possibility, but saying that his disciples should go beyond it, and turn the other cheek, give the extra cloak, walk the extra mile, and give to all who beg or borrow. Even so, what can he mean by saying that disciples should not resist evildoers? That we should let criminals get away with their crimes unpunished? Or does he mean that we should give beggars whatever they ask for? There is a variety of suggested interpretations for such statements. One, which seems quite plausible to me, is that he is using exaggerated statements for effect, which it would be absurd to take literally, but which remind us that we should not be vindictive. We should not look for immediate retaliation (even if we are legally entitled to do so), but should practice restraint and concern for the welfare of others, whatever the provocation.

This is just one possible interpretation. The point is that it is very difficult to find an interpretation that we can apply in our daily lives, and Christians differ in how they take the sermon. But it does seem to me that it would be silly to take these as rules to be literally applied by everyone. They rather seem to point to inner attitudes that should govern my relations with other people. But they do not say exactly what I should do in specific situations. Most Christians seem to agree with this when it comes to at least some of the sermon. When Jesus says, 'Do not swear at all' (Matt. 5.34), Quakers take this to forbid swearing an oath on the Bible in a court of law. But most Christians do not take Jesus' remark literally. They swear on oath, and explain that Jesus really meant to recommend complete truthfulness, not to ban literally swearing an oath. In other words, most Christians do not take a literal interpretation, but look for an underlying spiritual meaning, which they think (rightly, in my view) is much more important.

The Use of Scripture: 3. Jesus on Marriage and Divorce

At last I come round to mentioning sex, which I have deferred for as long as possible. Jesus says, 'Anyone who looks at a woman with lust has already committed adultery' (Matt. 5.28). The interpretation that seems most reasonable to me seems to fit this case very well. Jesus is talking about inner attitudes. We can interpret his statement as saying that anyone who inwardly desires a married woman has committed a sin which is a sort of adultery. But he goes on to say that if your right eye offends you, tear it out. That is certainly not literal. It is a hugely exaggerated statement to make the point that the nourishing of an active desire for a wrong (in this case, sex with another's wife) is itself a wrong. Then comes a very mysterious passage. 'Anyone who divorces his wife, except on the ground of unchastity (*porneia*), causes her to commit adultery, and whoever marries a divorced woman commits adultery' (Matt. 5.32). Divorce is allowed by Torah, and it was relatively easy for a man to divorce his wife, for 'indecency' (*porneia*), which could be very widely interpreted to mean anything shocking or unacceptable, not just adultery. But now Jesus says that if the man divorces a wife, it is she who commits adultery. This could only be so if she marries again, and so it seems to prohibit remarriage after divorce, even for women who do not want to be divorced, and who will be socially disadvantaged if they do not remarry.

This seems surprisingly uncharitable, if it is meant to be a rule. In some manuscripts, at Matthew 19.9, Jesus says, 'Whoever divorces his wife, except for unchastity, and marries another commits adultery.' This formulation is found in Mark and Luke also. That makes more sense, and at least puts the blame on the man.

Matthew certainly represents Jesus as saying that divorce is a bad thing, arising from human hard-heartedness. 'It was not so at the beginning' (Matt. 19.8). But is Jesus cancelling the biblical permission of divorce? Or is he rather saying (by analogy with the 'law of retaliation' case above) that divorce is permissible, but disciples should not divorce their wives? If we follow the analogy of that case, however, we might expect that this is not a specific rule, but that it points to an inner attitude. Just as you are not expected literally to let evildoers do as they wish without resistance, so you are not expected literally never to divorce, nor is a divorced woman literally guilty of adultery if she remarries. The point in the former case is to be non-vindictive, but what you are to do in specific cases depends on the situation. If the analogy is pursued, in the case of divorce the point would be to condemn an attitude of frivolity or lack of seriousness about marriage, and to encourage an attitude of loyalty to a partner 'for better or worse, until death'. Jesus would be pointing out that commitment to another in marriage is to be serious, lifelong and genuine, not a matter of momentary inclination or convenience.

But he would not be saying that in hard cases (as when a man deserts a woman), she is condemned never to remarry. Christian churches differ considerably in their interpretation of Jesus' reported remarks about divorce. The Church of England, strangely, has the harshest doctrine – that marriage is lifelong and remarriage after divorce is forbidden. Fortunately, perhaps, Anglicans rarely keep their own rules. The Roman Catholic Church also forbids remarriage after divorce, and holds that divorce is impossible, for marriage is indissoluble. This is a strongly literal interpretation of Jesus' teaching. But the Catholic Church nevertheless annuls many marriages, saying that they were not genuine, so in practice people can marry 'again', even while children of the previous 'non-marriage' still live. The Orthodox churches permit remarriage after divorce, as long as a public confession of regret for the breakdown of the previous marriage is made. Many Protestant churches permit divorce and remarriage, and so they are presumably committed to taking Jesus' words on this issue non-literally, as an exaggerated way of saying that ideally one should not divorce, and that one should do all one can to prevent divorce. But sometimes it happens, and we must then make the best of a bad job – and 'making the best' will often mean marriage to someone else. This shows how difficult it is to interpret Jesus' moral teaching on this central matter of sexual ethics, marriage and divorce. My own view is nearest the Orthodox and Protestant view on this issue, and for three main reasons.

First, Jesus' moral teaching in general seems to be stated in very exaggerated terms that cannot be taken literally, but that point to the ideal moral attitudes that should govern human life (we might think of Jesus' statement that a camel cannot go through a needle's eye as such a case, pointing out the difficulty, but not the absolute impossibility, of combining great wealth and Christian discipleship). So if we try to take one consistent way of interpreting Jesus' moral teachings, it has to be a non-literal way, but a way that does not undermine the importance of absolute moral commitment. The commitment will be, however, not to external acts but to inner attitudes. Such attitudes will normally issue in external acts of a specific sort. Lifelong commitment will normally issue in no divorce. But in hard cases, the required attitudes of true care for another and respect for their wishes can remain, or even be strengthened, by making an exception to the normal rules.

Second, Torah permitted divorce, as did all the rabbis of Jesus' day. The disciples may have been shocked at the severity of Jesus' teaching, but it was shock enough to them that he made divorce extremely difficult, when they were obviously expecting him to have a more liberal attitude (that itself is perhaps a clue to the general nature of Jesus' moral teaching. He was generally liberal or humane in his interpretations of Torah, arguing for healing and for picking ears of wheat on the Sabbath – both allowed by liberal interpretations of Torah, but contested by very conservative readings). And according to Matthew, Jesus did not mean actually to contradict Torah in his teaching.

Third, the literal interpretation of the divorce aphorism in the Sermon on the Mount would be uncharitable to innocently divorced women, and I cannot accept that Jesus' teaching was ever uncharitable. True love of neighbour will sometimes involve marrying, and taking care of, women who have been left alone through no fault of their own, or by a tragic breakdown of marriage. And it will sometimes involve letting a wife or husband go, when they do not wish to continue a relationship further. These are hard cases, and it would be a mistake to build a set of moral laws on hard cases. It is better to do as I, at least, believe Jesus did, and that is to set out the moral ideals that should govern human life, and leave hard cases to careful and particular consideration in often unforeseen situations.

The underlying principle that I would find in the Sermon with regard to sexual morality is that lifelong commitments of loyalty and trust, for better or for worse, are of great value, and should never be intentionally undermined (Matt. 5.31–32). In addition, it is wrong to make such relationships merely instrumental to gaining momentary pleasure, so that personal gratification is regarded as more important than a fully personal relationship of shared concern and experience (Matt. 5.27–30). Both these principles are fully consistent with love of neighbour, and they spell out what such love implies. In the form in which I have described them, they do not mention sex or gender at all. They are about friendship in general. And that, in my view, is how they should be taken.

The Development of Doctrine Beyond the New Testament

I have been concerned with one main problem in deriving moral rules from the Bible, the problem of interpretation. The other main problem is that of whether biblical moral teaching, even in the New Testament, can be said to be final or complete.

Christians differ completely from Jews in their interpretation of the Hebrew Bible. The books of the Old Testament, according to the Second Vatican Council of the Roman Catholic Church, in the document *Dei Verbum*, 'contain matters imperfect and provisional' (paragraph 15), and express 'the mystery of our salvation in a hidden way'. But if a God-authored scripture can contain imperfect and provisional material, suited to imperfect and provisional human understandings, this could in principle apply to the New Testament as well as to the Old. The Old Testament is said to be fulfilled in Christ, in whose acts and teachings the fulness of revelation is manifest. It might thus be the case that there are some New Testament writings – after all, often expressed in letters addressed to specific churches on specific issues of the day – that reflect an imperfect and provisional understanding of the theological implications of the acts

94

and words of Jesus. In fact this is almost certainly the case, on the strictest Catholic view.

The doctrines of incarnation and Trinity, for example, were not worked out for centuries, and are certainly not expressed with perfect and final clarity in the New Testament itself. With the completion of the New Testament writings, there was still much to be understood of the implications of Jesus' ministry and teaching. It might be said that this was a task entrusted to the Church. It is a task we can see being undertaken within the New Testament; but it surely continued beyond that, which makes the New Testament in one sense provisional. That sense does not undermine claims that in Jesus a final revelation of God's nature and purpose is given, or claims that the New Testament contains what God wished it to contain. But it means that the full implications of this revelation were not understood finally or with full clarity, even by the Apostles. We need to consider the whole Bible in its total range, with the life and acts of Jesus as the normative clue to understanding it, and with some knowledge of the Church's developing understanding of revelation that resulted in the dogmas of the great ecumenical councils from the fourth to the eighth centuries AD.

There are some sentences in the Gospels that, taken on their own, would give a very misleading account of Christian doctrines. For instance, in John's Gospel, Jesus says, 'The Father is greater than I' (John 14.28). And he also says, 'When the Advocate comes, whom I will send to you from the Father, the Spirit of truth who comes from the Father . . .' (John 15.26). These sentences imply that Jesus is less than the Father but greater than the Spirit, whom he has the power to send. Yet such a subordinationist view of the Trinity was formally denied by the ecumenical councils. These sentences were then given a very complex (and in my view unconvincing) interpretation to bring them into line with the later doctrine. They are good examples of biblical statements that need to be interpreted in the light of extra-biblical considerations to give what became an orthodox Christian view.

95

Paul and Freedom from the Law

I shall argue that the same is true of particular ethical rules cited in the New Testament. Many of them need to be interpreted in the light of subsequent Christian experience. If taken on their own, in a literal sense, they can be very misleading. This is not to say that New Testament ethical rules are of no importance. They do give some very clear guidelines to modern ethical decision-making. What I want to suggest is that in some important cases they do not give inflexible rules that cannot be amended, and that must be applied literally in the modern world. I shall show that no church takes all New Testament rules in such a literal sense. Indeed, there is the highest New Testament authority for refusing to take them in a literal sense, as binding rules for all time. That authority is Paul, whose views on the matter seem to be unambiguously clear. In the longest letter he wrote concerned with central issues of obedience to God's Law, revealed to Moses, he writes, 'Now we are discharged from the law ... so that we are slaves not under the old written code but in the new life of the Spirit' (Rom. 7.6). These are very strong words.

We are 'discharged from the law'. It has no binding authority for Christians, who are not bound by a written code. It is important to see that the Law, for Paul, was the whole Torah, including ritual, purity and moral aspects – including, as well as the rules for offering sacrifices, the Ten Commandments.

We are free of all of it. That certainly does not mean that morality has no force for Christians. Paul does not mean that the Old Law is not binding, and so there is no moral law at all for Christians. What he says is, 'Christ is the end of the law' (Rom. 10.4). Christ both negates and fulfils the written law, for he is in his own person the law (the Torah, the eternal wisdom of God) embodied. If we wish to know what Paul calls 'the law of Christ', we must look to Jesus' life and teachings. As we have seen, his teachings in the Sermon on the

Mount do not seem to lay down specific moral rules. But they lay before us a set of moral attitudes – of non-vindictiveness, truthfulness, respect for others, reconciliation and universal benevolence – that are rigorous and difficult. His life sets before us an example of healing, forgiveness, compassion, kindness, and care for those on the social margins. All these qualities can be brought to birth in us by the Spirit, and the life of the Spirit is a life whose inner attitudes are generated and sustained by the Spirit of Christ. The Christian moral life is one that pursues demanding moral virtues of character. But it is not one of obedience to specific written rules.

Paul writes that all the rules of Torah are summed up in this word, "Love your neighbour as yourself". Love does no wrong to a neighbour; therefore, love is the fulfilling of the law' (Rom. 13.9 and 10). We do often need particular rules, but their function is to spell out in specific situations what love of neighbour requires. If situations change, we might need different particular rules, but their justification will always be that they serve better to show neighbour-love than the rules we are trying to revise. Changes in circumstances, or changes in our understanding of what neighbour-love truly requires, may make revision of old rules morally necessary. 'If you are led by the Spirit,' writes Paul, 'you are not subject to the law' (Gal. 5.18).

The important thing, therefore, is to seek to be led by the Spirit of Christ, and then to ensure that our moral rules express this Spirit in the most adequate way. This suggests that the New Testament attitude to morality is most basically this: particular moral rules are revisable, but they must be revised to express the Spirit of Christ – of universal love and concern for others – more fully. If this is Paul's teaching, then we will naturally expect that, if Paul himself recommends any particular moral rules, it would be absurd to take them as necessarily binding for all time. That would contradict and wholly undermine Paul's own teaching. We should certainly take any moral rules Paul sent to the early churches seriously, and try to see what sort of instruction they might have for own lives. But in the end all such rules will be revisable, if a revision would enable universal love to be better expressed in different circumstances. It turns out that quite a few moral rules in the New Testament have been revised in this way through the centuries of Christian existence.

Six Cases of New Testament Rules Many Christians do not Keep

There are a number of moral rules that seem, as they stand, to express a very imperfect and provisional understanding of the universal love of God as it is seen in the life of Jesus. It looks as though some New Testament writers had not yet fully seen the radical nature of God's demand for universal love, and were still hampered by some of the limited social conventions of their own day.

Just as understandings of the Trinity are very imperfect in the New Testament, so are some moral understandings. If that is right, we can call on the fact that the Holy Spirit will lead us into all truth (John 16.13) by stressing that it may take a long time for the Spirit to get us anywhere near the full truth, and that the Spirit has to deal with some very limited and obdurate human hearts along the way. The New Testament letters give some examples of how human moral understanding, even when enlightened by the Spirit, was still limited and in need of further revision. The moral task is still incomplete, for we have still not understood the width and depth of God's demand for universal love, or what particular rules we need to express such an understanding. But the New Testament principle seems fairly clear – moral rules are always subsidiary to the principle of universal love, and we see better what that requires only as we reflect upon the life of Jesus and the active working of the Spirit in human hearts. I will give six problematic cases from the New Testament letters, where various churches reject or revise a literal interpretation, and where disagreements about interpretation persist in different churches, or even within the same church.

Food

First are the rules about food. As I noted, Acts 15 records the decision of a Church council to allow any food except meat with the blood in it, or food offered to idols. Paul, however, writes to the Gentile church at Corinth, 'Eat whatever is sold in the market without raising any question on the ground of conscience' (1 Cor. 10.25). Blood is now allowed, as it is for virtually all Christians to this day. This is a revision to the apostolic rule, reached as Paul himself struggled with the question of whether any foods should be forbidden. In this letter, he concludes that, since the Law has been set aside, the prohibition on blood too should be set aside. And he cites a positive reason – 'the earth and its fullness are the Lord's'. No wholesome food is forbidden to Christians, for it is a positive witness of freedom that no ancient taboos are binding. In this case it could be said that Paul too is an apostle – he certainly claimed to be, though it is doubtful whether he was ever commissioned by the other twelve. So his rule should stand. I do not deny that. My point is that we can see Paul continuing to think through the implications of true freedom in Christ. He even argues that food offered to idols could be eaten, since idols do not really exist, but that believers might refrain from eating it out of consideration for their weaker brethren, who might be misled into thinking Christians were worshipping idols. At least it is established that rules made by the Church can be set aside (at least by due authority) when circumstances make that appropriate. Here is a legitimation for the Catholic Church's view that the magisterium has authority to change moral rules – for example, in declaring usury legitimate after it had been earlier forbidden by the Third Lateran Council in 1179. For other Christians who do not accept such a central magisterium, there is legitimation for amending church rules, and for rejecting at least one New Testament apostolic rule (the rule about eating kosher meat). In this case, however, at least the revised rule (of eating anything at all) is clearly present in the New Testament.

Head Covering

The second case I will consider is one that is not contradicted or modified anywhere in the New Testament, but that most Christians now ignore. It is said that men should not cover their heads in church (unlike Jews), and that women should cover their heads in church (1 Cor. 11.6–16). Moreover, women should not wear make-up, visit a hairdresser, or wear jewellery or fashionable dresses (1 Pet. 3.3). Some churches take these rules literally, but most ignore them, perhaps suggesting a milder rule that women should not be obsessed with fashion or be ostentatious in parading their beauty. These, it may be said, are just matters of custom, not really moral matters. But they are rules suggested on New Testament authority. If they are rejected, the principle has been established that such rules are not to be automatically accepted. We can reflect on them, and decide that customs and conventions have changed, and they have simply become obsolete. How far can customs change, without undermining New Testament moral teaching? The Bible gives no rule for that, but it seems to me that the most consistent principle is to say that it is what underlies the rule that is important – the attitude of modesty and decorum. As social circumstances change, so particular rules on such subjects can change, as long as the underlying attitude is maintained.

Celibacy

The third case is one where different churches differ about whether to follow the rule or not. Paul teaches that it is better not to marry (1 Cor. 7), and in this he may seem to be following the teaching of Jesus (Matt. 19.11 and 12). Marriage is not condemned, but Paul thinks it is better to remain single, both because single people can work better for God, and because there is probably not much time left before 'the end'. The Orthodox and Catholic churches in general accept this rule, and the monastic or celibate life is held to be a special vocation for some Christians who feel called to perfection. Many Protestant churches, however, reject the monastic life, and even feel that it is better to be married than to remain single. If they do so, they are rejecting Paul's opinion. They may have good reason for that, but it would show that they think Paul's views on sexuality were limited or even mistaken at least on some matters – specifically, on whether marriage is to be preferred to celibacy.

That would open the way to other disagreements, if there were felt to be good reasons for revising an apostolic opinion. Paul also teaches that there should be no marriage after divorce – this, he says, is teaching from the Lord. Yet he says that a Christian can divorce his wife and remarry, if a non-Christian wife wishes to leave him (1 Cor. 7.15). He is not positively in favour of this, but is prepared to permit it – on his own authority, not that of Jesus, he says. It is ironic that Protestants, who claim to be more biblical than Catholics, often permit divorce and remarriage, but would not in general think unbelief a good cause for divorce. Even Catholics, who come closest to accepting this teaching literally, can only do so by saying that the dissolved marriage never existed in the first place. So no church quite keeps the rules in their strictly literal form, and churches differ about how strictly to be bound by the rule. I have suggested that Jesus did not actually forbid divorce, but held that it was morally undesirable. Paul can also be read in that way (and I would do so), but if so it should be clearly recognized that the moral rule is being taken as a moral ideal, and not a strict duty. That is, people ought to live up to it, but it is recognized that they may fail to do so, and then they may be given a second chance (that is, to marry again).

This is a case where churches differ considerably in their interpretations. The Roman Catholic Church does not accept the possibility of divorce at all, though many marriages can be annulled (declared never to have existed). Eastern Orthodox churches allow divorce and remarriage, but insist on a liturgical expression of penitence if remarriage takes place. Many Protestant churches allow divorce and remarriage. So there are major differences in the attitude of

Christian churches to these biblical rules, and it is doubtful whether any Church accepts what the New Testament rules literally enjoin – if, indeed, there is one consistent set of rules on the matter at all in the New Testament.

Slavery

The fourth case is one where all churches agree that the moral rules of the New Testament should be totally abandoned. These are rules concerning slavery, by which slaves are repeatedly told to obey their masters (for example, Eph. 6.5, and many other places). The New Testament nowhere teaches that slavery is wrong and to be abolished. Yet virtually all modern Christians would think that slavery is obviously wrong and contradicted by Christian teaching.

Whose teaching is this? It is not an explicit biblical rule. It is simply the implication, not explicitly spelled out, of unrestricted love of others. You cannot be said to love someone else if you can buy and sell them. There are one or two texts where slavery may be said to be implicitly condemned. The most obvious is Col. 3.11: 'there is no longer Greek and Jew, circumcised and uncircumcised, barbarian, Scythian, slave and free, but Christ is all in all.' Gal. 3.28 expresses the same thought: 'There is no longer Jew or Greek, there is no longer slave or free, there is no longer male and female, for all of you are one in Christ Jesus.' These texts, however, obviously cannot be taken literally, since males and females do not cease to exist in Christ. The meaning must be that barriers between slave and free, male and female, are broken down. But it is not quite obvious that there can be no slaves or that slaves are to be the social equals of free persons.

These texts may be taken to refer to inner attitudes of respect and care, but leave social institutions as they are. Indeed, I think that is correct. The institution of slavery, like institutions of sexual inequality, is not condemned in the New Testament. Rather, what we have to say is that in thinking through all the implications of new life in

Christ, and of unrestricted love for everyone, we come to see that slavery is incompatible with them, and the institution should be removed whenever possible. So we have to admit that the rules about slavery are provisional, and that it is a limitation of moral vision that leaves slavery intact, throughout the New Testament. The implication is that there may be yet much to be worked out about what unrestricted universal love implies morally. It may render many biblical moral rules obsolete, and deepen our moral vision beyond anything that is explicitly stated in the Bible.

Obeying the State

The fifth case is of something that again has not been thought through fully in every New Testament document. Paul writes that we should obey the state authorities, for 'those authorities that exist have been instituted by God' (Rom. 13.1). This may be true where the ruling authorities are fairly just, and where it could be plausibly said that they have been instituted by God. But what happens when Roman imperial law commands that sacrifices be offered to the emperor as to a god?

Christians were to discover many laws that could not be obeyed, and many authorities that should be resisted – like communist governments that ban the practice of religion. In a similar way, governments that legislate morally unjust laws – like the South African laws under apartheid – cannot be obeyed, at least in those respects. And dictators like Hitler cannot be obeyed when he commands persecution of the Jews. There are hundreds of cases where Christians should not obey the state authorities, and cannot believe they have been instituted by God.

What we can do with this rule is to say that it can be accepted within normal limits – given a fairly just government. There is a prima facie duty to obey the government, and that is not a trivial rule. Nevertheless, there is also often a duty to resist a radically unjust government, and the Bible does not tell us exactly when a government becomes radically unjust. We just have to decide that. What is needed to accept the rule is that it needs to be specified more closely, and exceptions to it need to be made clear. It is totally unacceptable simply to quote the rule from the Bible, and say that is what we must do in all situations. Sometimes it is right to contradict the rule, and resist a government. But as Christians we would need to have a good reason for that. And the reason would be to protect justice and institutions that promote universal unrestricted love among all people. We have here again a case in which the basic Christian principle of neighbour-love may require a contradiction of a specific biblical moral rule, in circumstances which make that rule inappropriate.

Male Headship

The sixth case is that of male headship. Paul writes that 'the husband is the head of his wife' (1 Cor. 11.3). The writer of the letter to the Ephesians says, 'Wives, be subject to your husbands as you are to the Lord' (Eph. 5.22). And the writer of the first letter to Timothy says, 'Let a woman learn in silence with full submission. I permit no woman to teach or to have authority over a man; she is to keep silent' (2.11 and 12). There are churches that keep these rules literally. Some Protestants clearly reject them, ordaining women ministers and sometimes working for full equality and reciprocity between men and women.

As in the case of slavery, these rules are consistent and clear throughout the New Testament. They are not contradicted anywhere. To abandon them is to abandon the principle that New Testament rules are morally binding on modern Christians. Not only are they not morally binding; they would be regarded by many, both Catholic and Protestant, as actually immoral if put into effect now. It is quite hard to find a more general moral principle underlying them. Some have tried saying that women should submit to their husbands, but men should also submit to their wives. This, however, is impossible. Two people cannot both submit to each other. Perhaps the best one can do is to say that partners should respect each other, regarding their wishes as more important than selfish desires of one's own. In cases of conflict, partners should try to come to a mutual agreement, accepting some principle that gives full and fair treatment to each over a period of time. Where there is irresolvable conflict, sometimes the woman's view should prevail, and sometimes the man's. It all depends on who is most reasonable, sensitive and responsible. For many Christians today, these rules just reflect primitive social conditions in which male headship was taken for granted, and the New Testament writers not only passively accepted these conditions (as, arguably, with slavery), they seemed enthusiastically to commend them to all.

This is short-sightedness and provisionality of a high order. Here are biblical rules which need to be excused, not justified. The excuse can only be that in a society where male headship was taken for granted, Christians were looking for the best way of living as lovers of God. If men took proper care, and had proper respect, for their wives, then their wives could submit without fear. It was a weak and passive view, but an understandable one, for people who did not want to shake strongly rooted social conventions.

But the most likely explanation is that they simply did not think about it. It just did not occur to them to challenge accepted thinking – just as it does not occur to many Christians today to challenge the accepted thinking that we can kill animals for food, when we do not need to do so. The New Testament does not propose any principles of specific political organization. Probably the first generation Christians did not envisage ever being in a position to change the political system that existed in their Rome-dominated world. Democracy and human rights are never mentioned. Such things have to be derived from more general principles that are only implicit in the text.

Is there a Christian reason for thinking male headship is wrong? Yes there is. The one simple and overwhelming reason is appeal to the principle of universal unrestricted love. It is that principle that, at least for a large number of Christians, overturns New Testament rules about gender relations. Men and women are certainly different, and they may well have emotional and behavioural differences that have been genetically inbuilt to sustain different rules in the generation of children.

Women, evolutionary biologists often suggest, are genetically designed to bear and rear each child for at least two or three years, and then to bear more children. Women will be more concerned with domestic virtues, and with qualities such as kindness and concern. Men, on the other hand, are designed to propagate children as widely as possible, without bearing responsibility for their upbringing. Their virtues are likely to be militaristic, brutal and disciplinarian. These gender-specific virtues were reinforced over thousands of generations in small hunter-gatherer societies.

But the social revolutions brought about by agriculture, by the rise of industrial societies, and most recently by the information revolution, have transformed the social conditions of human existence. Women can control or prevent child-bearing, and men do not have to spend weeks hunting for prey. The most important virtues are connected with intellectual abilities, and in this respect there are few, if any, genetic differences between the sexes. Even if there are differences in general (in spatial awareness, for example), these differences will not be expressed in every case, and there will be many exceptions to the general rule.

So gender differences are genetically conditioned, but have become either irrelevant or counter-productive in modern global societies. Insofar as we have freedom to vary our genetic traits, we need to counteract them. It is thus because of the new social conditions under which humans live that gender differences that were codified under the principle of male headship now need to be modified. We now need a principle of mutual responsibility. Men and women can learn to take responsibility for child-rearing and for providing food and clothing. Many women are stronger and more intelligent than many men, and many men are weaker and less able than many women. In a rational society, the leader should be the more able, whatever the gender. So we can have women presidents or prime ministers, who can make the time to devote themselves entirely to political matters.

Old genetic patterns will not be changed even in a few generations. But new cultural patterns can channel them in more rational ways. Gender differences are genetically entrenched. Gender equality can be culturally reinforced. The issue is thus one of inherited and pre-rational behaviour versus rational organization. Insofar as Christian morality has a view of gender, it might well prefer to be on the side of reason and responsible control of purely material (genetic) behaviour, to prefer the rule of reason to the rule of passion. And so far as it is, it will recommend gender equality.

To love all others means to respect and care for all, including partners of the opposite sex. Respect for persons means being concerned for the interests of others, working with them and treating them fully as responsible intelligent agents. That is the principle that renders obsolete the New Testament conventions of gender preference.

One difficulty felt by many today is that Jesus was a man, and he chose only men as apostles, though he had many female disciples. This may seem to support the dominance of masculinity, and the Church has often taken it to do so. But we should bear in mind that in the social conditions of his day, the Messiah had to be male to be considered a king of Davidic descent. The apostles had to be male, to be accepted as peripatetic prophets of the kingdom among their contemporaries. In other words, their gender was constrained by the social roles available at the time. Social conditions have now changed out of all recognition, and have made those constraints obsolete. If gender truly is spiritually irrelevant, then it does not matter what gender Jesus and the apostles were. They could have been either, except for the social conditions of a specific society. So now, when social conditions are quite different, it follows that they could be either. And in a society where there is a moral struggle to establish the full and equal personhood of women, it becomes important to ensure that gender equality is affirmed in every social context, that the Church leaves no social role unattainable by women.

On this issue, differences will remain between those who follow the biblical rules as literally as possible, however inappropriate they seem in modern society, and those who appeal to the underlying principle of respect for persons, however much it undermines one specific class of biblical rules. The latter will say that the gender of Jesus is spiritually irrelevant. What matters is his character as loving and reconciling and caring especially for the socially less privileged. If we take these features as determinative, we will say that it is a Christian duty to affirm fully female equality, especially in church. For the Christian gospel affirms that all persons, especially the poor and outcast and socially excluded, can participate in the life of God. There is no privileged class or spiritual elite in heaven. So it should be on earth. Perhaps, then, those who follow the Bible most truly are those who are prepared to abandon specific biblical rules where they have become opposed to a fuller expression of a truly Christ-like appreciation of the full stature of every human person, of whatever race, colour, creed or sex.

Homosexuality

Modern social conditions have transformed our thinking about gender and sexuality. Christians are faced with a new situation that the Bible never envisaged. Sexual relations have become separable from the procreation of children; women are not destined to a life of child-bearing; men do not have to be the protectors of and providers for the rearers of their children, who in turn do not have to be enclosed to prevent their insemination by other sexually promiscuous men. We need to rethink our sexual morality in accordance with the principle of universal love, guided by the moral ideal of a life of joy in God, of compassion, and realization of the talents God has given us. Important biblical principles that remain are those of commitment to lifelong loyalty in friendship, and to respecting the full autonomy of others.

Clearly there will be sexual sins. Intercourse with animals or young children is wrong, because it does not express love and concern for the responsible freedom of others. Adultery will be wrong because it breaks up partnerships. Promiscuity and pornography are wrong because they disconnect sexual pleasure from any fully personal relationship. Thus an important Christian principle is that sexual intercourse should express a fully personal, and not a fleeting or impersonal, relationship. This is because our bodies exist to express our personalities, and should not be misused by subordinating personal to purely physical ends. What might be called the 'personalist principle' is that all our responsible bodily activities should serve to express personal excellences such as kindness, compassion, co-operation and creativity. Further, persons exist only in society, so our personal relationships should be such as always to reinforce friendship, trust and reconciliation. Such relationships are very fragile, and so institutions like that of marriage build areas where we can be sure of fidelity and concern, whatever happens, and where children can be brought up in an atmosphere of love and kindness.

However, things can go very wrong in marriage, and for that reason divorce, while always regrettable, has to be accepted as the least bad option for marriages that become destructive of love and compassion. Moreover, if lifelong friendships are good, and if procreation becomes divorced from sexual expression, and if there are people who genuinely are attracted to partners of the same sex, the way is open to the recognition of Christian same-sex partnerships.

Homosexual sins will be, like heterosexual sins, those of promiscuity, unfaithfulness and pornography. These are the sexual sins condemned in the New Testament. 'Be sure of this, that no fornicator or impure person, or one who is greedy (that is, an idolater) has any inheritance in the kingdom of Christ and of God' (Eph. 5.5). The

Greek terms translated here as 'fornicator' and 'impure person' are *pornos* and *akathartos*, which might be translated as 'promiscuous' and 'dirty-minded'. If the body is the temple of the Spirit, it must always be used to express respect and love, and to build up those qualities of mind and heart that will cement and not destroy social relationships. Promiscuity and vulgarity do not do this, and so are considered wrong.

Paul gives a similar list in his first Letter to Christians at Corinth: 'Do not be deceived! Fornicators, idolaters, adulterers, male prostitutes, sodomites, thieves, the greedy, drunkards, revilers, robbers – none of these will inherit the kingdom of God' (1 Cor. 6.9 and 10). Here three more Greek words are added: adulterers (*moichoi*), male prostitutes (*malakoi*), and sodomites (*arsenokoitai*), literally 'adulterers', 'soft people', and 'sleepers with males'.

Adultery is plainly wrong, by undermining a long-term relationship. 'Soft people' may be those who are addicted to sexual activity, or (as in the NRSV translation quoted here) male prostitutes, condemned because they divorce sexual activity from personal relationships. It would be apposite to take 'sleepers with males' to refer to those who resort to male prostitutes, and to condemn their activity on the same ground, namely, that of sexual activity not conducive to building up personal relationships, and putting the pursuit of pleasure before the pursuit of distinctively human excellence.

These are representative of New Testament texts that condemn homosexual behaviour. It is noteworthy that the homosexual acts referred to are condemned alongside greed, theft, drunkenness and libel. These are acts that use others as means to one's own pleasure or that are concerned solely with the fulfilment of one's own desires in ways that undermine personal responsibility. That suggests that homosexual acts are wrong insofar as they pander to personal desire, ignore the rights and human dignity of others or undermine social relationships and responsibilities. They need not be taken as condemning same-sex relationships that are responsible, and that express and help to reinforce and build up a long-term relationship of love. I imagine that such same-sex relationships of friendship and love existed in New Testament times, as they exist in all societies, and that the question of whether physical sexual acts were performed within such relationships was simply not raised. Paul's concern was to oppose the pagan practices of sexual promiscuity and prostitution, and perhaps more widely to oppose the inordinate pursuit of physical satisfaction, in a way that undermines the pursuit of fully personal and social goods. In many modern societies contraception is practised, gender roles have become more fluid, and biological knowledge has advanced to the stage at which same-sex attraction and the diversity of sexual preferences is acknowledged. In such societies I see no reason why same-sex love should not be accepted on the same conditions as heterosexual love. I doubt whether it falls under Paul's condemnations. I also doubt whether he ever seriously considered the issue in such terms. If so, then the acceptance of homosexual partnerships is less in contradiction to New Testament rules than is belief in the equality of the sexes.

The real issue with regard to homosexuality probably lies in our genetic tendencies to encourage heterosexuality as conducive to procreation. This conflicts with a less prevalent, but still strong, tendency to same-sex attraction (because of the fact that sexuality is not an all-or-nothing factor, but covers a wide range of possibilities). There is a genetic battle under way, which sometimes even becomes explicit – a genetic tendency to abhor all acts that do not encourage procreation versus accepting that human gender covers a genetic continuum from male machismo to effeminateness, from female motherliness to tomboy temperament. As far as the rational control and direction of human genetic inheritance is concerned, the time has probably come to take sides with the more polymorphous character of sexuality, and seek to ensure that physical sex is always governed by the principle of Christian personalism; the use of the body in all its activities to be an expression of the distinctively human excellences of mind and spirit.

Conclusion

There probably always will be Christians who regard the New Testament as preserved from error by the Holy Spirit, and who seek to apply its moral rules in a literal way. I have shown, however, that even then there are many ways in which interpretations may diverge, and that very few churches manage a wholly consistent application of biblical moral rules.

I then suggested that examination of the Gospels and the letters of the New Testament uncovers something important about the character of Christian revelation. It is given, not in a written law, but in the person of Jesus. Jesus' teaching is cryptic and challenging, and seems more focused on inner attitudes than on specific rules. The letters contain passages that have not moved beyond conventional moral views, with all their limitations. We might expect continued reflection on moral issues to lead to deeper insights into what Christian love requires.

Christian moral thought should refer to the Bible, but must make new moral decisions as new circumstances come into being, and is not wholly bound by literal application of biblical rules. Christian moral views vary from the more conservative – applying literal rules as nearly as possible – to the more liberal – seeing the underlying principle of neighbour-love, as exemplified in Jesus, as overruling some specific biblical rules. The New Testament gives a very incomplete account of morality, failing to deal with issues of political organization, warfare, issues of life and death and of human rights. For that reason alone, it is unsatisfactory to regard it as a complete moral system. So one may reasonably take it as conveying a set of basic principles, mostly concerning inner attitudes, which have to be worked out in new circumstances by personal moral decision. In that sense, Scripture would have authority as laying down the sort of human excellences God requires, but not as a set of moral rules one cannot revise or discard if necessary. Christian Scripture would not be a 'law of God'. It would rather be a set of witnesses to the revelation of God's nature and purpose in Jesus, and that would be complemented by the attempt to live in the power of the Spirit which comes through the community of disciples, the Church.

The tension of ancient revelation and contemporary creativity remains, but the revelation becomes more like a matrix for a set of attitudes than like a set of laws. Christianity is distinctive in being a religion of the Spirit of the living Christ. Creative change is near its heart, and its main ethical principle is to seek to discern the Spirit of Christ, understood imperfectly even by the apostles, in the very changed circumstances of the contemporary world. It has to be admitted, however, that not all Christians see it like that. The desire for unchangeable God-dictated laws is strong, and the disturbing wind of the Spirit is not easy to accept. My argument has been that a truly biblical morality is one that is open to, and that sometimes positively calls for, creative change. For the God revealed in Christ is a God who calls us to move beyond ancient rules into the creative life of the Spirit. Paul said, 'For freedom Christ has set us free. Stand firm, therefore, and do not submit again to a yoke of slavery' (Gal. 5.1) – not even, we might say, slavery to the moral rules of Paul.

The Christian religious tradition does provide important moral insights into human existence and sexuality. It stresses the dignity of human nature, the importance of long-term relationships of loyalty and faithfulness, openness to the long-term care of children within a loving relationship, and the necessity of a fully personal dimension to all sexual relations. Yet social conditions have changed considerably in the modern world, and the specific moral rules of ancient societies may no longer be applicable. So specific rules must often be changed by consideration of what makes for true human fulfilment. They should always be ordered by reference to seeing such fulfilment in relationship to a God of mercy, compassion, justice and love.

Unthinking insistence on ancient rules may be an abandonment of the deeper religious principle of discerning the will of God for human fulfilment in a rapidly changing world. But the underlying principles of love, loyalty, fidelity and the integrity of the human person are the unchanging principles that it is the task of religious faith to bring to human morality.

5

Respect for Life:
Buddhism and Questions of Life and Death

I may seem to have taken for granted that religion is about conscious relationship to God, and that the main moral issue to be discussed when reflecting upon morality and religion is the relation between the will of God and human decision-making in morals. My general argument has been that religious morality does not primarily consist in the revelation of new and specific moral rules – we have a natural knowledge of right and wrong without religion. The idea of God provides a transcendental dimension to morality – it roots morality in an objective reality of supreme goodness, love of which can motivate us to greater moral effort, and encourage us to hope for the eventual realization of universal human fulfilment. But there is one major religion for which the idea of God has no special importance. That is Buddhism, which generally rejects the idea of a creator God and the importance of conscious relation to such a supreme being. There is no God to issue a set of moral commands, and there is no question of humans simply having to obey those commands, whether they want to or not.

Yet while there is no God, in the sense of a creator of the universe, in Buddhism, there are Buddhas, Enlightened Ones, who, by long practice of meditation, moral striving and intellectual discernment, have come to see the final truth of existence, have been liberated from suffering, and have entered into *nibbana*,[1] a virtually indescribable state in which there is full understanding and bliss. Gotama

---

1 I have transliterated the Pali term as 'nibbana', whereas the more familiar 'nirvana' is from Sanskrit.

was just one such Buddha, and he is the Buddha for our world and age. His authority is as absolute as the authority of God, for he knows the truth and the way to liberation, and what he teaches springs from his own experience of enlightenment, the true goal of every human life.

Many Buddhists will say that Buddhism is not an authoritarian religion, and that its truths are to be experienced personally. But how many of us have experienced *nibbana*, have been freed from sorrow, and discern the true nature and meaning of existence? Most Buddhists will say that very few have done so, and perhaps in the last few thousand years Gotama is the only one to have done so. Because of that, we must accept his authority as incontrovertible. It is true that personal experience is the ultimate test of truth. But our experience is vastly inferior to that of Gotama. Therefore the Discourses of the Pali Canon have absolute authority for those who wish to walk in the way of enlightenment. Buddhist Scripture teaches the final truth about reality, and derives from a source that knows such a truth by its own experience, and is inerrant. So it turns out that most Buddhists accept scriptural authority in just as full a sense as any Abrahamic believer in divine revelation.

One of the most influential of all Buddhist authors, Buddhaghosa, a fifth-century CE Sri Lankan scholar, says, 'Scripture is incontrovertible. It is equal to the First Council in authority, and is just as if the Buddha himself were alive today' (*Commentary on the Monastic Rule*, i, 231). The First Council was, by tradition, a meeting of senior monks held shortly after the Buddha's death, in the fifth-century BCE, and it is held to have established the canon of Buddhist Scripture, known as the Pali Canon. It must be said that most non-traditionalist scholars do not regard this tradition as plausible, as the texts of the Pali Canon were only committed to writing in the first century BCE, about 400 years after the Buddha's death. The Pali Canon consists of three main collections of texts, the Discourses (teachings and sermons of the Buddha), the Monastic Rule (*vinaya*) and the Scholarly Treatises (*abidhamma*).

The best known part of the Canon, a work that is short, readable, and provides a beautiful poetic exposition of Buddhist teaching, is the *Dhammapada*. But the Discourses as a whole are important as providing teaching that is said to be the teaching of Gotama himself, on various occasions during his ministry after he had reached enlightenment.

I should make it clear that I am mostly speaking of Theravada Buddhism, the major form of Buddhism in Thailand and Sri Lanka, which has a good claim to have remained fairly close to the original teaching of the Buddha, so far as that can be ascertained.[2] There are many forms of Buddhism, and it is impossible to deal with them all. So what I want to do in this chapter is to concentrate on some elements of Buddhist doctrine, as it is found in some Theravada schools. The other major form of Buddhism, Mahayana, or 'the greater vehicle', has its own scriptures. They were mostly revealed to various sages by direct inspiration from a Buddha or Bodhisattva in another spiritual realm. The most popular such scripture in East Asia is probably the *Lotus Sutra*. Again its authority lies in the fact that it has been reliably received from a being who is omniscient at least with regard to everything concerning human liberation. This form of Buddhism is closer in many ways to theistic beliefs, but it is not the form of Buddhism I shall deal with.

The Buddha's Ethical Teaching

The Buddha's ethical teaching is not a set of revealed commands. It is advice on the way of life that leads towards the attaining of enlightenment. The nearest thing to commandments are the Five Precepts for lay Buddhists. They are: do not take life; do not steal; do not misuse sex; do not lie; and do not take intoxicants. These are guidelines

---

2 Good introductory texts are: Peter Harvey, *An Introduction to Buddhism*, Cambridge; Cambridge University Press, 1990, and Richard Gombrich, *Theravada Buddhism*, London: Routledge, 1988.

for the sort of conduct which keeps one compassionate and mindful, and leads towards non-attachment and the ending of suffering. For some Buddhists, the higher states of consciousness are 'beyond good and evil', in that once the goal is attained, the way to it can be dispensed with. There are forms of Tantric Buddhism in which moral rules are intentionally broken to demonstrate one's freedom from passionate desire. But mainstream Buddhism insists on conformity to high moral standards – primarily, however, as a training of the mind in non-attachment and liberation.

There is no set of moral commands that are to be obeyed without question. There are guidelines, rooted in the experience of advanced spiritual teachers, for attaining liberation from suffering. The primary strength of Buddhism lies in its practice, a practice leading to the liberating experience of that reality of compassion, wisdom and bliss which is *nibbana*. So Buddhism differs from the Abrahamic faiths in being primarily a practice aimed at liberative experience, a discipline for achieving a spiritual goal. The Abrahamic faiths appear more as a revelation from a living personal reality, God, who is to be worshipped and obeyed. Yet this simple contrast between the two traditions is blurred and complicated by the fact that many later Buddhist traditions include a strong devotional element (to Amida Buddha or to compassionate Bodhisattvas), and the goal of the Abrahamic faiths is often said to be union with a reality beyond literal description, having the nature of wisdom, compassion and bliss, possible only for those who have overcome egoistic desire. This suggests that the approaches of the Abrahamic and the Indian ascetic traditions may be more complementary than contradictory.

Buddhist ethics is based on the personal authority of the Buddha, which is held to be enshrined in scripture. Nevertheless there are very few specific moral rules laid down in the scriptures. Since Buddhism has traditionally been primarily a monastic movement, there are many rules for monastic practice, and some ethical rules can be generalized from them. But the general Buddhist attitude is that one should not be 'fettered' by too great an attachment to specific rules. It is better to uncover the underlying principles or mental attitudes, and then to see how these can be best expressed in differing social circumstances. Such underlying principles are capable of being interpreted in a very rigorous sense, and it should not be thought that they lead to any sense of moral indifference on the part of Buddhists. On the contrary, Buddhist morality is principally a discipline of the mind in the virtues of compassion and loving-kindness, and such virtues clearly rule out some actions – one cannot be compassionate and steal another's property, for instance. The ethical question for Buddhism is just how rigorous or absolute the specific moral rules that follow from the general principles are to be – and that is analogous to a similar question in theistic religions. In my discussion I will concentrate on what is without doubt the most basic ethical principle of all in Buddhism – the principle of respect for life, which includes rules concerning abortion, embryo research, and euthanasia, that could be generated by basic Buddhist principles. As the Emperor Asoka said in his Brahmagiri Rock Edict: 'One should respect the supreme value and sacredness of life.'

He does not speak, as Christians tend to do, about the sacredness of human life. He speaks about the sacredness of all life. Buddhists seek to extend their sympathy and compassion to all sentient beings, all beings capable of feeling pleasure and pain. There are other religions of Indian origin that go even further. The Jains hold that all things are filled with souls, and one should seek not to destroy anything that exists, for one is thereby harming countless souls. The principle of *ahimsa*, non-violence, which so much influenced Mahatma Gandhi, is a key Jain principle, that Buddhists would also accept. It teaches that one should not kill or even harm any living thing – and perhaps everything that exists is in some sense living. As a 'middle way', Buddhism does not go that far, and on the whole when its Scriptures speak of 'life' they tend to speak of 'sentient beings', beings capable of feeling pleasure and pain.

The Doctrinal Texts analyse human life into five *khandhas* or groups, which are named as *rupa* (material or physical form), *vedana* (feeling, or sentience, the capacity to experience pleasure and pain), *sannya* (cognition or perception, including the recognition and classification of objects), *sankhara* (will, volition, or the cluster of dispositions that give rise to karmic causality) and *vinnyana* (discriminative consciousness, including basic awareness and discrimination of its basic aspects). This final quality is also known as *citta* (mind or heart or possibly the connecting thread of personal continuity). These collections of qualities are difficult to translate precisely, and commentators dispute about how exactly they should be described. It is agreed that they together form an assembly which is the human person, and that there is no further continuing 'self' or person that stands over against them or 'owns' them as its own experiences. The human self is simply the collection of these qualities. It is this collection, or at least the karmic consequence of its actions, that is 'reborn'.

In the state of final release, the collection dissolves. But it does not dissolve into annihilation – a view the Buddha explicitly disavowed. It rather dissolves into a higher unconditioned state of cognition and bliss, a state beyond the realm of *samsara*, of personal desires and accumulating karmic consequences. The stream of human consciousness has, it may be said, been transfigured into the unconditioned state beyond division, attachment and suffering. It becomes – or realizes that it always has essentially been – a Buddha, free of all finite limitation, one with the unconditioned.

Human existence has a special importance for traditional Buddhists, since only in such an existence can liberation be achieved. But rebirth in many forms is possible – humans can be reborn as animals, and animals as humans. So it is important to respect all living things, since they either have been or will be human, and compassion is appropriate for them, since they are involved in the realm of suffering.

It looks as though the five *khandhas* are arranged in order of complexity. All material objects have bodies or material form. All animals have perception or some ability to feel pain or pleasure.

Perhaps only some animals can recognize objects and have cognition. Perhaps only humans have volition, and become capable of morally relevant acts of will. Discriminative consciousness, insofar as it is a fluid 'sense of continuing self' (though it is in fact a complex bundle of mental states), will also be characteristic of humans.

It seems that it is because humans possess the complex properties of will and discriminative awareness that they become capable of liberation, and can play a positive role in affecting their karmic destiny (or the destiny of those beings whose arising depends upon their volitional acts). But living beings will be anything with the capacity to feel pain or pleasure, and with primitive cognition. Such beings are worthy of respect, and the First Precept enjoins that their lives should not be taken.

I confess that after all the violence and killing that sometimes seem to characterize the Abrahamic faiths I feel something of a sense of relief at finding a religion that condemns all taking of life, and enjoins the extension of human sympathy and loving-kindness to all living beings. There is no scriptural excuse here for hatred or violence against others, and excessive attachment to one's own beliefs or creed is explicitly condemned in the Pali Canon.

Respect for Life and Human Rights

It may look as though no further discussion of abortion, embryo research, euthanasia and suicide is needed, when considering Buddhism. They all involve the taking of life, and are therefore morally prohibited. Yet morality is never as simple as that, and modern medical progress has raised issues that are not addressed in the Buddhist scriptures. It is those issues I propose to discuss. I make no pretence of discussing the complex differences on ethical issues between contemporary Buddhists, or of providing a complete survey of Buddhist ethical thought. Instead, I will try to make the discussion manageable by concentrating on one excellent treatment of the subject by Damien Keown,[3] who has defended the rigorist view that indeed all taking of life under the above heads is prohibited. This will enable me to look at the main ethical issues of respect for life from a non-theistic religious viewpoint, which has a distinctive view of what a human person is, and I hope that will prove to be illuminating for those to whom such a viewpoint is unfamiliar.

Let me begin, then, by asking the most basic question for Buddhists: are there conditions under which the taking of a life is morally justified? The obvious justification is self-defence, either against an animal predator, like a tiger, or an aggressive human. Most Buddhists would accept such a justification, though in the scriptures soldiers who die in battle are said to be reborn in hell or as an animal. If an aggressor threatens to kill large numbers of innocent people, it will save lives overall if the aggressor is killed (if there is no other way of resistance). So 'Do not take life' is not an absolute rule. There are exceptions, and there are grey areas, where lives saved and lives taken have to be balanced against each other.

We do not want to say that we can take a life whenever we thereby save more lives, since that would justify killing healthy people to distribute their organs to a number of ill people. So taking life is justified only against an aggressor, one who actively desecrates the sanctity of life – and this is probably true whether the aggressor consciously intends to kill or not. We might shoot a mentally impaired, and thus not responsible, person who was about to explode a bomb to kill many innocent people.

The Beginning of Life

This case is relevant to the question of abortion. For it implies that we could take the life of an embryo if it threatened the life of the mother – and many Buddhists accept this. Buddhists often regard

---

3 Damien Keown, *Buddhism and Bioethics*, Basingstoke: Macmillan, 1995.

the offence of abortion as increasing in gravity with the age of the embryo, and that seems to imply that embryos become 'more human' as they develop. If a living being is one that has the capacity to feel and perceive, such a capacity does not exist before the development of the brainstem, which cannot be dated before six weeks after conception.

To 'have a capacity' does not entail that the capacity is actualized. I have the capacity to play the violin, but I am never going to exercise it. But I do not have the capacity to fly; that is not possible for a being like me. So a three-month-old child in the womb may have feelings or perceptions of a very primitive sort. Its capacities will be very limited, but these are undoubtedly the capacities of a living being. Without a brain, a being cannot have such capacities, and in this fact lies a reason behind the natural feeling that very young embryos are not fully human persons. They do not possess human capacities.

This suggests that Buddhists should be able to countenance abortion before the stage at which embryos develop a brain. In fact, most Buddhists regard abortion as cutting off a 'precious human rebirth' that is widely taken to begin at conception. But with a greater knowledge of human embryology, there is some reason to think that Buddhism allows or even could encourage a different view. There is an early text (*Vinaya* iii, 73) in the Monastic Rule, which reads: 'A human being [exists] in the interval between the first moment when mind arises in the mother's womb, the first manifestation of consciousness (*vinnyana*) and death.'[4] This suggests that a human being exists only when discriminative consciousness exists. Such consciousness implies the existence of actual perception, feeling and volition. So it implies that a human being comes to exist at a fairly late stage in embryonic development. Before that state the embryo is due the protection given to an animal and, before a brain exists, the protection given to non-sentient life.

---

4 Trans. I. B. Horner as *The Book of the Discipline*, 6 vols., Pali Text Society, 1938–66.

On the Buddhist view, souls (collections of karmic elements) wait for embodiment between births, and they descend when a suitable material body has been formed, to constitute that collection known as a human person. Presumably such souls descend at a specific time, and some account must be given of when that time is. Keown argues that conception is the only justifiable time for such a descent. This is because he insists that 'the view that the moral worth of a human being arises and disappears as [a specific set of capacities] come and go is an idea which finds no support in Buddhist sources'.[5]

Humans are complexes of mental and material elements with a history and destiny which transcends a single lifetime. Keown quotes Buddhaghosa as saying, 'The very first moment of existence in human form consists of that first moment of mind (*citta*), with its three associated immaterial components [that is, feeling, thought and character] and the body of the embryo which is generated along with it' (*Commentary on the Monastic Rule* ii, 437). For Keown, mind binds together the five collections of qualities into a unitary whole. In this sense, minds exist through many thousands of rebirths. At any particular birth, they wait for fertilization to take place, and then associate with the fertilized ovum to produce a new human life. Mind precedes body, and the moral status of mind does not change through time, depending on how its capacities are manifested or restrained.

The thought of souls waiting for rebirth probably does give rise to the belief in much popular Buddhism that human life is indeed to be dated, in its physical manifestation, from the moment of conception. But that does not seem to follow from a Buddhist belief in rebirth. We now know in much more detail about the origin of human life, and this enables us to be more precise about the early details of human genesis. When an ovum is fertilized, a packet of DNA is formed, which will govern the form of the body and at least the general dispositions and capacities of the mind (the ways in

---

5 Keown, *Buddhism and Bioethics*, p. 29.

which the emerging person will tend to think, feel and act). DNA is a code, inscribed on long molecules, for constructing such an embodied person. Such codes can be stored in frozen cells, and placed in ova from which a previous code has been removed (in cloning, for example) and subsequently implanted in a womb.

Such frozen DNA cannot be called a person, though it is certainly human material, for it exists in every cell of a human body. It is a genetic code that will never naturally function as a code. When it is placed in an ovulating cell in a laboratory, such a cell will divide to form a small ball of identical cells, but will then inevitably die. A dividing ball of cells cannot be called a person. Again, the code is simply not translated. It is just a chemical code. This seems closely analogous to an ovum fertilized through intercourse which fails to implant. A new DNA code is created, but it is not translated into an organic form. This suggests that fertilization is not a reasonable point at which to say that a human person exists. The code for a person exists, but then every human cell in every human body carries such a code. The fact is that the conditions for its operation do not yet exist.

Keown points out that before fertilization there is no one individual that will develop into a person, and after fertilization there is such a genetic individual, with a distinct set of 46 chromosomes. So, he says, fertilization marks a point at which a new individual comes into being. It would be more exact to say that when 46 chromosomes of the right sort come to exist in an ovulating cell, by whatever method (intercourse or laboratory technology), they form a distinct code for developing a human organism. If the process is normal, that code will be replicated in a vastly increasing number of cells, linked in a developing organism. Strictly speaking, that original cell does not continue to exist as an individual. It generates many qualitatively identical individuals, linked organically. All that remains the same is the code, instantiated in a number of linked but undoubtedly new individuals.

This way of looking at the matter agrees with the general Buddhist tendency to deny individual continuance, and insist on the transient existence of all individuals within a continuing but ever-changing process. The creation of a specific DNA code is a crucial event within the process of human genesis. But it is no more crucial than the differentiation of cell functions, the development of a central nervous system and brainstem, the emergence of sentience, or the ability to exist independently. Something new, but in developmental continuity with what already exists, occurs at each of these stages.

If what is morally important and crucially distinctive, for a Buddhist, about human life is its capacity to generate or eliminate karmic consequences, then the morally crucial stage will be that at which such a capacity properly originates – quite late in embryonic development. If that never happened, there would exist no truly human life, however much genetic qualitative identity there was between earlier and later stages in the process. It does not seem as if the creation of a new genetic code in an ovum is, for a Buddhist who does not believe in substantial continuity of any sort, either a morally or an ontologically crucial event. It is part of a continuous process, and we have to decide how to treat entities within that process in accordance with what they really are (or should be) at a particular stage. If and only if the ball of cells (blastocyst) created by fertilization is implanted in a womb, it will begin to develop, gradually taking embryonic form.

Now the code begins to be translated into an organic form, as it builds protein from its environment. After about 14 days the central nervous system begins to form (this is the 'primitive streak'), then the brainstem forms, and electrical activity can be detected in the brain after about six weeks. This is also around the time at which the embryo was traditionally said to be 'formed', or to have a discernible bodily shape.

It seems to me that when Buddhaghosa wrote of mind and body being generated together, this is the moment that best fits his description – though that is admittedly not the traditional view in Buddhist societies like Sri Lanka. Of course it is not a datably precise moment. The development of the embryo is a continuum, in which new properties gradually emerge. But there is some point at which the first consciousness occurs in a growing embryo, however indistinct or elementary it is.

We might well wish to place the inception of a human life early in the continuum, but the principle is that without the capacity for consciousness or mind, a properly human life does not properly exist. There is a code for constructing a human life, but that code does its constructing piece by piece over a period of time. Why, then, should Keown prefer to think of fertilization as the origin of fully human life? He thinks of a human person as a complete integrated 'bundle', no part of which is the 'real essence' of personhood – certainly not 'rational thought', for instance. For then we might regard humans who could not think rationally as subhuman, and that is a conclusion rightly to be feared. But it is not the case that the various parts of the human bundle are inseperably integrated. For Buddhists, parts of the bundle – the immaterial parts – can exist without bodies, since souls exist between rebirths. Since humans can become animals, volition and conceptual thought may also be stripped from the bundle during an animal existence, presumably to be reunited after the animal's death.

Human existence is valued by Buddhists precisely because volition and reflective thought, which produce karmic merit or demerit, only fully exist in a human life. So I think Buddhists do distinguish some qualities as more important and as more human than others, and they do regard humans as special because of specific qualities of volition and reflection that humans possess. Keown himself says that only 'life with a moral biography' – roughly, life offering a chance of liberation – has intrinsic value. Other, non-human, life has only instrumental value.[6] This plainly marks out some forms of life as morally important because of the distinctive properties of volition they possess.

---

6 Keown, *Buddhism and Bioethics*, p. 49.

But sentient non-rational life does have intrinsic value. Health and happiness are, I would think, intrinsically good for animals, and therefore intrinsically good in themselves. But they are much less good than the capacity for moral self-shaping and for liberation that fully volitional and reflective beings possess. For Buddhists, there is an obligation to promote the health and happiness of animals. They cannot be wilfully destroyed. But there is a greater obligation to respect and promote the morally responsible agency of which humans are capable.

It may be the case that all animals have been, or will be, human persons. But that does not mean it is appropriate, for example, to treat cows as humans. They should be treated as sentient beings, with compassion but not with respect for a moral agency that they do not, in their temporary form of existence, exhibit. 'Life with a moral biography' – volitional and mindful life – is given a special moral status in Buddhism, even though compassion for suffering should regulate our dealings with all sentient beings.

Abortion

It is important to say that the moral worth of a human being does not vary with the presence or absence of rational abilities. We do not want to say that some people are subhuman, or only partly human. What we need in order to make such a moral point is a distinction between deficiency and potentiality. A person suffers from a deficiency if they lack something that it is natural for them to have. A person has a potentiality if in the future they may come to have a capacity, but it is not natural for them to have it yet. We may hold that in a compassionate society, which a Buddhist society would be, there is a special duty of care for those suffering deficiency in some human good. Those who are mentally or physically deficient are deserving of more compassion and moral concern, not less. But if people have potential capacities, it would be silly to treat them as though they had actual capacities (to let children vote, for example).

Potentiality is nevertheless an important property. If something is a good, and a being has the potential to realize that good, such a being should be sustained and not killed. One reason for not killing an embryo is that it has a natural potential for becoming a rational person. However, this seems to be what some call an 'imperfect', not an 'absolute', duty. That is, if X is a good, it will, other things beings equal, be good to promote it and whatever leads to it. But it does not follow that it is always wrong to frustrate processes that would naturally lead to X. There may be circumstances in which such processes also lead to great evil, or which prevent the realization of other goods. In the case of abortion, the most obvious cases are those where birth would lead to the death of the mother, or to grievous physical or mental distress, or to the child being unwanted, neglected or abandoned.

Buddhists regard human life as a good, in the sense that it allows the possibility of liberation. But they also regard life as an evil, in that it necessarily involves suffering and death. They hold that the highest form of human life, as a monk, will not involve procreation at all. So human life is not unequivocally good, and there is no obligation to procreate as many human lives as possible, or even as often as nature might incline one to.

Compassion is appropriate for living things, precisely because they suffer. Simply killing them would not help, since their karma has to be worked out one way or another. And killing would usually cut off the possibility of positive goods like perception, health and happiness. But it is not regarded as good just to increase the number of living beings. Ideally, it would be better if there were no living beings in the realm of *samsara*.

This suggests that, while taking sentient life is forbidden in Buddhism, there is no absolute obligation to refrain from terminating a being with the natural potential for sentient life – that is, a pre-sentient being in a human womb. Any of the reasons just mentioned might be sufficient to defeat any such obligation. From this it follows that the use of artificial contraceptives or such things as the

129

'morning after' pill are readily justifiable, though they do need some justification. This may be given by reference to such things as world population problems, the ability to care for children responsibly, or even the ability to provide a good quality of life for the family and society.

It is not true to say, as Keown does, that 'the decision to use contraception becomes a choice against life in that it deliberately frustrates its coming into being'.[7] Such a decision does prevent a birth, as does abstinence from intercourse. One can frustrate a good as effectively by refusing to have sex as by having sex using a contraceptive. But the decision to prevent a specific life from coming into being is not a choice against all such lives coming into being. It may be wise to frustrate a possible good sometimes, if thereby one prevents an evil, and one is not frustrating all goods of that kind.

A positive choice can be made for life that can flourish, and for the good of all life on earth, and it may entail wise family planning. Moral obligations in this area, for married couples, seem confined to producing life that can be reared happily and well. Indeed, if procreation was the only good to be considered, marriage would have little importance. Marriage exists to enable children to be reared safely and happily, and that entails not simply having as many children as possible. It is not life or even human life as such, in any form, that is an intrinsic good. It is life as a necessary condition of other goods, such as knowledge, friendship and happiness – and above all, for Buddhists, the possibility of liberation, the attainment of supreme knowledge and happiness.

It is not unreasonable to hold that abortion before the onset of sentience has the same moral status as artificial contraception – the prevention of a physical process the natural consummation of which is sometimes the existence of a human life. We have to say that the consummation is 'sometimes' a human life, because it is estimated that between 30 and 75 per cent of fertilized embryos fail to implant,

---

7 Keown, *Buddhism and Bioethics*, p. 129.

or if they do implant, are spontaneously aborted without the mother even knowing they were there, usually because of some genetic defect.

Like many physical processes, like fertilization itself, this is one where a large number of attempts are made, most of which will fail, in order that a few might have a chance of achieving the goal of reproduction. It is not like a process that tends directly towards a goal. It is more like a process that scatters shots in all directions, so that some of them have a good chance of reaching a desired goal. It is a stochastic or probabilistic process, with a very high probability that most attempts will fail, but also a rather lower probability that one of them will succeed.

Most fertilized ova will not generate human lives. Some of them, sooner or later, will. So the question is: what sort of moral consideration would you give to a being that has a small chance of generating a human being, by a combination of its own internal development and a favourable environment? The answer may depend upon how much you want a human being. Moral problems only arise significantly where a human being is not wanted – in cases of rape, for instance, or of unwanted conceptions in an already large family that can hardly be supported. It seems that in such cases there is no obligation to preserve a non-human being that has a small chance of becoming human. However, when it becomes sentient, its chances of developing consciousness also become very high, and there arises an obligation not to eliminate it – a level of obligation roughly equivalent to our obligation to sentient animals. It may seem callous to regard early embryos as animals. But from a Buddhist viewpoint animal life is to be respected. In addition, a bodily and emotional link has been established with the mother, which is morally significant. And it is hard to say when higher mental functions become established exactly – so it is probably better to err on the side of caution. For these reasons, a sentient but not yet fully human life is entitled to a high degree of moral care, and should not be eliminated for trivial reasons.

Yet a properly human obligation only begins with the origin of discriminative consciousness. Keown quotes the Zen master Robert Aitken as saying that decisions about abortion lie with the mother, and if, fully compassionate and mindful, she decides to have an abortion, 'there is no blame, but rather acknowledgement that sadness pervades the whole universe, and this bit of life goes with our deepest love'.[8] This view may be, as Keown says, a peculiarly Zen and Western one, but it perhaps reflects the better knowledge of embryology we now possess, the general availability of methods of safe abortion, and a Buddhist attitude to moral precepts as guides rather than unbreakable absolutes. If such a view is accepted, there is no moral problem with embryo research, with using stem cells for therapeutic purposes or for research. For such cells are taken from genetic material that will not be implanted, and that has not yet begun to develop any cell diversity of structure and function.

A problem that does arise is whether fertilized ova with an identified genetic defect (like Downs syndrome) should be terminated, in favour of ova that are 'healthy'. The implication is that this is permissible, until a fully human life has come into being. It is therefore a matter of great practical consequence at what point one considers a life to be fully human. This is a matter on which views, religious and non-religious, differ, and there seems to be no way of resolving them. We can only seek to know all the observable facts as fully as possible, seek what seem to us to be the most appropriate analogies to and counter-examples for the view we hold, and try to see all the consequences of our decision. We must then decide as well as we can how far our analysis is coherent with our general view of human nature and of the nature of ultimate reality. I have set out a moral view on these issues that I think a Buddhist view of human nature would suggest. But I am not suggesting that all Buddhists would agree, and the really perplexing fact is that I can think of no way of resolving these issues decisively. In this respect, ethics is

---

8 Keown, *Buddhism and Bioethics*, p. 102.

like religion, and we have to live with the need to make some vital decisions in a situation of theoretical uncertainty.

Euthanasia

There is, I have suggested, a general Buddhist view of human nature as not containing any one continuing self or individual entity, and of moral precepts as guidelines for conduct conducive to the development of those mental states that lead to liberation. Traditional Buddhists must allow for the rebirth of 'souls' (bundles of properties) in physical bodies, and hold both that karma will inevitably work itself out, and that it is better not to be reborn. Despite Keown's carefully argued view, I think this naturally suggests that there is no obligation to procreate, that frustrating a process leading to birth is not always morally wrong, and that there are identifiable basic properties of life that make it morally valuable – sentience and the capacity for responsible volition and reflective thought. Beings may possess such capacities even though they do not exercise them, and their impairment by some pathology does not mean that such capacities do not exist, as those of a fully human entity. So there is no license in this view for treating humans with latent or impaired capacities as less than fully human.

The Buddhist principle of respect for life, while it is wider in range than typical Abrahamic principles (in that it extends to animal life as well as human) is less absolute than at least the Catholic principle that an innocent human life should never be directly terminated, even from the moment of its conception, nor should a natural process leading to its creation be frustrated. For Buddhists, what constitutes a human life is a more fluid notion, and there is no moral obligation to 'be fruitful and multiply' (Gen. 1.28). In short, while we must have compassion for all sentient beings, there is no absolute moral principle that a human being should never be killed.

This means that for a Buddhist there may be no absolute prohibition on euthanasia, in the sense of assisted suicide. The most obvious cases are where there is extreme pain without hope of recovery, where someone is progressively losing all volitional and cognitive mental functions, or where a person is in the most severe persistent vegetative state. If human death is defined by analogy with the origin of human life, the most appropriate definition of death will be that of neo-cortical brain death. When the neo-cortex ceases to function, there can be no volitional or cognitive, no 'karmic', processes.

This differs from brainstem death, when the brainstem ceases to function. Then bodily functions like respiration or reflex responses cannot continue without artificial aid. Keown rejects neo-cortical death as a criterion for ceasing to regard beings as human persons, because of his belief that a human being is a total, integrated psycho-biological unity. He sees neo-cortical death as a state in which the human being still exists, but has in extreme cases lost one of its capacities – the capacity to be conscious. But it seems to me that a more natural Buddhist description would be that the spiritual properties have departed, leaving only the 'home of consciousness' (*Samyutta Nikaya* iii 9)[9] from which the home-dweller has departed forever. We would not treat an abandoned home as we would a home with a person in it.

Further, many comatose patients require technological help to keep them alive – tubes, enemas and catheters. The problem becomes acute when very expensive medical techniques are required to keep alive a body with no possibility of consciousness. Keown suggests that there is no duty to treat complications that arise for such patients, though they should be given food and water. It seems to me, however, that there is no duty to prolong the existence of a body with no possibility of consciousness. But I recognize that opinions will continue to be divided on this matter. It is an empirically unresolvable, but morally decisive, question.

A major argument in Indian traditions against suicide is that karma must work itself out; suicide is no escape from karma, and

---

9 Trans. C. A. F. Rhys Davids and F. L. Woodward, Pali Text Society, as *The Book of Kindred Sayings*, 5 vols, 1917–30.

such suffering as there is must be experienced sooner or later anyway. This argument does not apply where consciousness has ceased to exist. But it would apply where a patient is in extreme terminal pain. A Buddhist may say that pain is not evil, because it is the necessary working out of bad karma. But this would lead to the conclusion that pain should never be relieved, which seems unacceptable. Compassion requires the alleviation of pain wherever possible. So if there is terminal pain, without the possibility of remission or of being counterbalanced by some other sort of mental good, it should be alleviated, even if that causes death.

That is not a direct taking of life – though the distinction is often a very fine one. But there are extreme cases – for instance, a soldier dying in agony after a fatal injury who asks to be shot – where killing is the only way of ending the pain. Perhaps it still makes sense then to say that your intention is to end the pain, but it looks as though killing is the means (the only means) to end pain. In such extreme cases, which do arise, it might be regarded as permissible to take a human life, since the extremity of the pain renders any reflective volition impossible, and so the possibility of volitional karmic action by the sufferer has effectively ended.

The criterion in such cases is whether any reflective volition is possible. If extreme pain renders it impossible, and if there is no possibility of remission, then killing could be seen as an act of compassion, and so permissible for a Buddhist. Keown objects that it is still the taking of a life, and so the deprivation of a good. But is life, as such, a good? It is certainly the necessary condition of any other good, as is consciousness. For without life and consciousness, we could not be aware of any state or activity as good. But both may also be necessary conditions of evil states, like extreme pain. In such cases, life might be said to be, not an instrumental good but an instrumental evil, a necessary condition of an evil state.

Human life is certainly not a supreme good for Buddhism, since the whole point of the Eightfold Way is to cease being reborn as a human. It is only good, therefore, as an instrumental good, as a necessary condition of cultivating virtuous mental states. Patience and endurance may be such virtuous states. But if the higher mental functions of volition and discriminative consciousness are lost, a virtuous life is no longer possible. In such extreme cases, life is no longer even an instrumental good. In such cases, especially when there is extreme pain, compassion may lead one to end a human life, on the grounds that it is not life, however agonizing, that is to be respected, but rather the living discriminative consciousness which will, on Buddhist theory, not be wholly terminated by bodily death.

A case that is much less clear is the decision to take one's own life to avoid an inevitable process towards senility or total lack of independence, so that one may die mindful and self-possessed, rather than demented or confused. It is good to die self-possessed, but on the other hand there are still virtues of mind that can be exercised even when one is wholly dependent on others, and a senile person can have a painless, even happy life. So there is much less justification for euthanasia in such cases. Nevertheless, some Buddhists at least feel that the quality of volitional consciousness may become so restricted that one is living at best with the properties of sentience and perception only, as the higher animals do. There remains a requirement to respect sentient life, so it would still be better not to commit suicide. But if the condition is one that brings great distress, suicide could be seen as a personal decision that is understandable, if not commendable.

Absolute Moral Precepts

Buddhist scriptures deal with a primarily monastic discipline to root out attachment and attain liberation from desire and suffering. They have high authority for most Buddhists, and they certainly enjoin a set of moral precepts that include a prohibition on the taking of sentient life. But modern ethical issues surrounding the beginning and end of life were not considered in the scriptures, and there are different ways in which scriptural teaching might be used to address such issues.

Damien Keown argues for the position that a human life originates at conception and ends with brainstem death, and may never be directly terminated either as an end or a means to some other end. But I have suggested that the Buddhist doctrine of conditioned co-origination, or the lack of a substantial central self or person, does not support such an argument. It seems rather that all sentient life is to be valued, insofar as it offers possibilities for happiness. And human life is to be especially valued because it is a volitional and reflective form of life that may lead to liberation (even if individuals may not use, or may not be able fully to use, their capacities). This suggests that human life begins with the first functioning of the neo-cortex, and ends with the cessation of such functioning.

Further, the doctrine of absolute, unbreakable moral rules may seem to be foreign to the Buddhist dislike of fixed attachment to ethical precepts. So the precept forbidding the taking of life may be overridden by other moral considerations, especially compassion for those in pain or experiencing avoidable suffering. Keown's position is reminiscent of the Roman Catholic doctrine that respect for life is an absolute moral prohibition. But it may be doubted whether prohibitions on taking innocent human lives or on telling lies are quite absolute. There may be special circumstances – which admittedly need to be carefully defined – in which moral precepts may conflict, and cannot both be obeyed.

I know, for instance, that lying is wrong, because being deceived is rationally undesirable by any rational being. I may wish not to be deceived, in general, but I may want to be flattered on occasion, and I certainly do not always want people to tell me the blunt truth. There may be many occasions on which I do not mind being deceived for a good reason (for instance, when a big surprise party is being planned for me). So I can rationally break the precept not to lie to others, if that sort of reason can be produced.

The same holds for taking human life. There may be occasions on which I would no longer desire life, even though I agree that life is good in general. Then the Golden Rule would permit me to take life when there exists a rational desire to die. There may be other prudential reasons why I should not have such permission (such as the danger of misuse of such a principle for selfish ends). But at least the arguments would have to be taken seriously.

Appeal to natural law, in the sense of universal knowledge of right and wrong, seems to lead, not to absolute but to prima facie prohibitions. A prima facie prohibition is one that holds unless there is some other moral principle with which it conflicts. Then one of the prohibitions in question is overridden. One would expect the prohibition on taking life to outweigh the prohibition on lying. But it may be impossible to state rules about weighing moral judgements that will hold in every possible circumstance. In this way, natural moral knowledge is unlikely to lead to absolute prohibitions that allow absolutely no exceptions, whatever the circumstances.

This is not the official view of the Roman Catholic Church. Pope John Paul II, in the encyclical *Veritatis Splendor*, written precisely to combat 'probabilism', the opinion that moral rules are not necessarily absolute, writes, 'Only a morality which acknowledges certain norms as valid always and without exception for everyone, can guarantee the ethical foundation of social coexistence.'[10] I have to say that is simply not the case. There can be strong foundations for social morality in a set of prima facie moral precepts, that all can see to be right in general, though conflicts are possible between such precepts. Ethical decisions are often difficult and agonizing, precisely because we have to weigh different sets of moral considerations. It is quite possible to insist on the moral importance of precepts like not killing, lying or stealing, without adding that such precepts can never conflict or be overridden in extreme cases by stronger precepts.

---

10 *Veritatis Splendor*, 1993, para. 97.

Thomas Aquinas seems in at least one text to have taken such a view. In the example Aquinas takes,[11] natural law can tell you that it is right to return goods held in trust to their owners. But by itself the law cannot tell you in specific cases, where special conditions may obtain (the owner may be about to use the goods to attack one's country), whether it is right to return goods or not. 'The general law admits of exceptions' under special conditions. This is most obviously so when divine commands override natural law (as when God commanded Abraham to sacrifice his son). But it may also be so 'on some particular and rare occasions'. In the instance cited, the law against theft is overridden by a precept to prevent loss of life. In a similar way, many hold that the law against lying can be overridden by the precept to prevent murder. Though contemporary Roman Catholic moral theologians may not allow such exceptions, Aquinas himself plainly did.

We may agree with Pope John Paul that 'without intrinsically evil acts, it is impossible to have an objective moral order',[12] but add quite consistently that there can be degrees of wrongness (lying is less grave than killing), and that there are genuine moral dilemmas, when intrinsically evil acts conflict. It then becomes obligatory to do the lesser wrong. We would of course have to interpret the word 'intrinsic' as meaning 'wrong in itself, not just because of its consequences, except in cases where it is overridden by a greater wrong'. This might be called a weak interpretation of the term 'intrinsic'. But that is an intelligible interpretation, though it is not the same as the strong interpretation of intrinsic, namely, 'without any exceptions at all'. It is precisely because there is an objective moral order that we can assess the relative gravity of various moral prohibitions, and determine never to violate a moral prohibition except in cases where it is overridden by a stronger prohibition.

It seems to me that the present Roman Catholic position on absolute moral prohibitions does not depend solely on human

---

11 Thomas Aquinas, *Summa Theologiae*, 1a 2ae, question 94, article 4.
12 *Veritatis Splendor*, para. 82.

reason or natural law. It is a matter of revelation, depending for its force on the teaching authority of the Pope. For those who do not accept that the teaching of the Pope is morally binding in conscience, the defence of absolute moral prohibitions is, I think, not possible.

Since Buddhists do not accept the Pope's teaching authority, they have little reason for believing in absolute moral prohibitions. And if moral rules are primarily means to attaining the primary Buddhist objectives of the relief of suffering and the attainment of liberation, then the right to life, even though it is a central and important Buddhist belief, is not absolute. It may sometimes be subordinated to the need for compassion.

Not all Buddhists will agree with this assessment, by any means. This reinforces the point that on such complex moral issues there is not one agreed religious viewpoint, even within one religious tradition. Perhaps Buddhism is right in holding that the primary concern of religion is not the resolution of moral dilemmas, but the teaching of a discipline aiming at liberation from egoism and union with a reality of supreme compassion, wisdom and bliss. Unresolvable moral issues are not a province in which religion has a special authority, or to which it can offer a universally acceptable solution. Such things we each have to work out to the best of our ability, or by accepting the authority that seems to us – and the element of personal judgement is inescapable – to be the most reliable. At least I think this is the view of morality, and of questions of human life and death, that seems most coherent with the world-view of Buddhism.

This view could also be accepted by many believers in God. For the fundamental issues are the same: is it life as such, whether God-given or not, that is to be respected absolutely and unconditionally? Or is it life as the condition of sentience, understanding and creative will, that is to be respected in various ways, depending on the capacities that various conditions of life make possible?

Religious views do not give one answer to these questions. But religion does see human life as a gift and a responsibility, and does insist that respect for life, however difficult to interpret in hard cases, is a categorical demand. In a world in which human life is often treated with callous disregard, morality needs all the help it can get from religious faith, even if religious faith sometimes needs reminding that respect for life is one of its own most basic principles.

6

Religious Laws and Human Freedom:
Torah and Talmud

In writing about the relation of religion and morality, I have argued that the basic elements of morality are knowable by human reason without religious revelation. This is a very widely held view in the world religions. The role of religion is to give backing to moral ideas by affirming the existence of an objective reality in which moral values are fully realized (God, for example), and which can motivate and provide hope for the final success of human moral endeavour.

But are there not specific religious laws, given by God, that humans have to obey whether they want to or not? Is it not the case that, in Judaism and Islam, for example, morality is not a matter of human decision but a matter of divine command? And does that not limit the area of human moral decision-making, and place humans under unquestioning obedience to a set of divine commands?

In this chapter I shall consider the Jewish Law, the Torah, as a system of divinely revealed statutes and ordinances, and ask how it relates to systems of secular law that are based on purely human decisions. Critics argue that religious law is archaic and oppressive, and that humans must be freed from its constraints. I shall examine such claims, and my general argument will be that Jewish religious law can be and should be fully humane, and in fact that it has important insights and lessons for secular legal systems. I shall also develop a specifically liberal interpretation of religious law, and argue not for its universal adoption, which would be absurd, but for its acceptance as a responsible and appropriate interpretation of religion for the twenty first century.

The Structure of the Hebrew Bible

Abram (if, the critical historians would say, there was such an individual) possibly left Ur in about 1800 BCE, sometime after the Sumerian Third Dynasty had come to an end. The exodus of the Hebrews from Egypt, which may again be partly legendary according to many historians, could be dated to around 1235 BCE. If so, some of the laws of Moses could date from around that time, towards the end of the Bronze Age in the Middle East, and could be seen as forming a combination of Hammurabi's interest in moral codes with Akneten's monotheism, to produce the first real form of ethical monotheism in history.

However, this is all rather speculative, and the extent to which the Hebrews were really monotheists at that time is much disputed. The Bible records a continual struggle to sustain belief in the one God of Abraham, Isaac and Jacob. It was not until 1075 BCE that the Semitic people developed a true alphabetical script, and the earliest reliable written records in the Bible, from a historical point of view, are the court chronicles of Kings David and Solomon (who probably did exist), dated to about 1000 BCE. Most scholars think that it was much later that the main writings of the Hebrew Bible, traditionally divided into the Law, the Prophets, and the Writings, were edited into something like their present form. Many would estimate that the first five books of the Bible, which form the written Torah, the Law of God, were not compiled in their present form until after the return of the Israelites from exile in Babylon, in the mid-fifth century BCE.

The Orthodox Jewish view that the Torah was given to Moses and that at least part of it (Genesis–Deuteronomy) was written down at Sinai, or at least during the life of Moses, has to be a matter of faith, not evidence. To a non-Orthodox historian it seems more likely that the Torah was built up gradually over centuries.

The creation account, for example, is thought by many scholars to be one of the last parts of the text to be written, and there seem to be various sets of laws dating from different centuries that have all been set alongside one another into an edited account after the exile. Some historians doubt that Moses was an actual individual, and think of him as an imagined source of the whole complex collection of laws that were gradually collected together into Torah.

In giving an account of the history of religious thought, we have to note here, as has to be noted in virtually every ancient religious tradition, a difference between traditionalist believers and critical historians. Traditionalists hold that a sacred text, in this case Torah, was verbally given to a prophet or seer, and then passed down without error or change by oral tradition over many generations. Later Orthodox rabbinic thought held that Torah is eternally existing, and that the earthly Torah is a copy of the eternal Law of God.

Critical historians – and it must not be forgotten that many, perhaps most, religious believers are not traditionalists as I have defined them – think that the Hebrew Bible developed orally over many centuries, and incorporates many diverse viewpoints, some of which scholarship is able to identify. They were edited in a written form that became canonical or official Scripture. They may in some sense be inspired by God, but they were not dictated by God, and they are unlikely to have been passed down unchanged for many generations. Only when they were written down did they become fixed, and even then there remain many possible interpretations of the texts, which often contain incomprehensible or ambiguous passages, conflicting traditions, and variant readings in different manuscripts.

The traditional Orthodox view is that not only the written Torah, but also the oral Torah, which was passed down by word of mouth, was given to Moses at Sinai. For an Orthodox Jew, the Tanach or Hebrew Bible, which Christians call the Old Testament, is certainly important. There are three main sorts of inspiration for a traditionalist view of the Hebrew Bible. The Torah was dictated to Moses by God. The prophets were inspired by God, who spoke through them.

And the writers of the Psalms and Proverbs and other writings were also inspired by God, though in a more general way (not usually by dictation or possession by the Spirit of God). But for Jews, the Mishnah, or 'Instruction', is equally important, as it is the oral law given to Moses. It was not finally compiled in written form until the third century CE, and forms part of the Talmud, which contains laws on many topics, together with commentaries and discussions (Gemara). Talmud is in practice of great importance to Jews, and forms the chief object of study in the Yeshiva, the religious schools. In it there are recorded many rabbinic debates as to how the laws should be interpreted and applied in various circumstances.

The Nature of Torah

There are two features of Talmudic study that may surprise those who are unaware of Jewish religious practice. First, Torah is not just a set of commandments (613 of them by tradition). There are statutes and ordinances, Mitzvot, but these are set in the context of the historical narrative of the patriarchs, the exodus and the journey to the promised land. Torah is not just a set of laws. It is a history of the relation of a covenanting, liberating, guiding God and a particular group of people. The covenant is a calling by God, a promise by God to remain present to the people, on condition that they follow the way that leads to life and thereby become the priests of the earth and a light to all nations. The Law is for human good; it is a way that leads to life and to relationship with God. It is not like a set of arbitrary commands. It is the path of life, and obeying the Law is responding in personal trust to a liberating and life-giving God.

By contrast with the Upanishads of Indian tradition, the Torah does not explore the nature of God. It presents a narrative of the acts of God, within which the way that people are to follow to relate to God is made clear. The Law is a path of relationship to a personal creator. While the being of God remains always ultimately

145

mysterious, hidden in the cloud of divine darkness, the way that humans are to take in order to find life in God is revealed. Because of this, interpreting Torah as Law can be misleading. It may suggest a legalistic approach, where the laws are obeyed for their own sake. Whereas the laws are obeyed because that is how to show complete trust in God, and how to establish a living relation with God. In short, the laws are not just to be obeyed, but the giver of laws, who is the creator of all things, is to be loved, and the laws show how to do that.

The second feature of Torah is that the laws are not just to be taken literally and applied at face value. They are, in rabbinic practice, to be debated, argued over, interpreted in various ways, and enacted in different circumstances by judicial decision. The second main part of the Talmud, the Gemara, is largely written in the form of discussions in which different opinions are canvassed, and different legal decisions are noted.

There is a variety of ways in which the Talmud can be regarded by religious Jews. Going through all the possibilities exhaustively would indeed be exhausting, but it may be useful to list six main attitudes that exist somewhere within Judaism. It will turn out that something like this range of attitudes exists in many religious traditions, and thus seems to be a characteristic property of religious understanding. Diversity seems to spring essentially from the claim to possess a sacred scripture that needs to be interpreted in many different contexts. It is perhaps one of the most important facts about a revealed religious law that it essentially breeds diversity, not unanimity. It is a chief peculiarity of religion that even while this is true, Scripture is often presented as giving a way to overcome diversity and present one normative set of beliefs or practices. That is perhaps the central self-misunderstanding of religion. A great advance might be made in religious understanding if it was acknowledged that diversity is both inevitable and positively good.

Interpretations of Torah

The following outline of the diversity of religious Judaism might help to make this point clear:

1A For some conservative rabbis, many legal issues are now closed (they were closed by early medieval legal decisions), and an exhaustive knowledge of past discussions and decisions, together with marked piety, is what is required of a leading scriptural scholar. Tradition is required to interpret the commandments, and an exhaustive knowledge of tradition is required before a rabbi is qualified to do so. But in fact most interpretations were established long ago, and innovative interpretations are not now possible.

1B Other Orthodox schools, however, hold open the possibility of new legal interpretations, which may rescind old decisions, if new situations or new knowledge seem to demand revision. Again, only qualified scholars have the authority to do this, and there can be various scholarly schools who accept rather different legal decisions, within a core of generally accepted interpretations. Both these schools can be called traditionalist. There is an interpretative authority for dealing with sacred texts. But the fact is that there are disputes about who exactly that authority is.

2A With the availability of a written text that can in principle be read by all, a new school of thought arose, rejecting the authority of the scholarly elite. Appeal is made to private interpretation of the text, free from any past interpretation. Of course, this widens the range of possible interpretations enormously, and in Judaism there is no central authority to decree that one set of interpretations is correct. One school of interpretation chooses the most literal reading possible, and insists that the laws should be applied as nearly as possible in their written form. This is very much a minority view, but it cannot be wholly ruled out.

2B A further possibility is that Torah is given a much more allegorical or 'spiritual' interpretation. One would look for underlying principles rather than specific binding rules, which are seen as meant for a specific time and society. In practice this might mean that Torah is distinctive mainly in family and religious matters. This 'privatization' or spiritualization of Torah contrasts with the opinion that Torah should govern the whole of Jewish public and political life, and it opens up a wide area of non-religious decision-making and law that is not under religious control. It is perfectly possible to be an observant Jew and accept the authority, within its limits, of a secular Jewish state like Israel, that legislates by democratic vote, and not by direct appeal to Torah.

These two views (2A and 2B) may be called scripturalist. They do not accept the need for a central interpreting authority. The text can be interpreted directly by readers. The text itself is taken to control the interpretation, but in practice there are many different ways in which it is read. Again in practice some interpreters are taken as authoritative, even where the right of private interpretation is emphasized.

3A Reform Jews take the principle of finding underlying principles in Torah further. They wish to give Torah authority, but do not feel bound by a literal obedience either to written Torah or to ancient rabbinic tradition. Torah functions as a source of meditation and inspiration, but does not replace the need for creative ethical decision-making, which seeks to obey the spirit, rather than the letter, of Torah.

3B More liberal or 'progressive' Jews may not regard the Talmud as binding at all, except as a pious adherence to tradition. This view may be called progressive (this word is not meant to connote moral superiority), and tends to view scripture as a cultural resource, but not to give it supreme authority. Its main problem is to say if any form of authority exists within Judaism, and whether there are any limits to the possible revision of past traditions. In practice, however, the scriptures are still publicly read, and so are regarded as having some sort of authority, even if that is an authority of an inspirational rather than an obediential sort. A text has inspirational authority if it is used as a source to inspire new insights in a specific group, to orient their general attitudes, to provide a source of discussion, and to record a tradition of historical development. A text has obediential authority if it is taken as a set of rules that are to be followed without deviation. Progressivists reject the text as having that sort of binding authority. On no view is unanimity obtainable, except within sub-groups that accept one authority as decisive – but there are always groups that reject that authority.

Diversity in Religion

This rather idealized survey of differing religious attitudes to Torah raises the question of whether unanimity is a reasonable thing to look for in religion. What is wrong with diversity? It looks as if, on all these views, the scriptures are taken to possess some form of authority, and some interpreters are given greater credence than others. But a variety of interpretations exists, and it does not seem that one set is clearly more justifiable or reasonable than others. To this extent, internal pluralism – acceptance of a diversity of possible interpretations – seems to be entailed by any dispassionate view of Jewish religious life.

A range of attitudes to Torah exists within Judaism, and it is clear that what characterizes Judaism, even Orthodox Judaism, is diversity rather than unanimity. It is agreed that Scripture largely takes the form of Law, and that observance of Law is central to Judaism. But after that, almost anything goes. Who you take as an authority, how binding you take that authority to be, and how free you are to make your own decisions, is in practice up to you – depending partly, of course, on what is allowed by the society in which you live at the time. There is, then, no universally agreed interpretation of the Law, and no single authority that can issue a 'guaranteed' interpretation. The point is that interpretations have to be made.

As with any living law, it is never enough just to repeat what was said hundreds of years ago. Law has to be applied; decisions have to be made; and who makes them, and who listens to them, varies widely within religious Judaism. Judaism is internally pluralistic. This is bound to be true of any tradition that relies on an ancient scripture which stands in need of interpretation. Disputes are bound to arise about whether the scripture has direct Divine authority, or whether it is a human construct, even if guided by a Divine hand; and about how it is to be interpreted, whether with greater or less adherence to ancient decisions. The fact is that scripture may be an essential guide to modern decisions about how laws should apply today, but those decisions have to be made on a non-scriptural basis, and then the question is rather one of deference to tradition versus private interpretation than of textual literalism. As a matter of fact, it is scriptural literalists who are non-traditional and 'modern', since the possibility that everyone should read scripture for themselves is historically speaking rather recent, and the choice to read scripture literalistically is a very non-traditional choice.

When scripture is passed on orally, there has to be a small elite of those who memorize the texts, and so scripture and its interpretation is controlled by them. With the invention of written script, authoritative interpretation is still confined to those who can read, a fairly small proportion of most early societies. The Jewish interpretation of scripture requires years of study of written sources, and the cultivation of the ability to judge between diverse interpretations in the Talmud. So the tradition relies on a relatively small group of scholars, though they divide into different groups, who take their lead from one sort of interpretation.

With the spread of literacy, the scripture becomes available to the majority. This has only happened since the sixteenth century, and is even now not universal. But it means that scripture escapes from the scholars. The irony is that many generally literate people have no training in religious thought, and just take the scripture literally or at face value, and without knowing the diversity and history of developing interpretations. So with widespread literacy comes a great increase in religious naivety, and also the growth of scriptural literalism. Non-traditionalists do not have to be liberal, and many of them today are not. Some combine religious ignorance, socially conservative attitudes, and a mistaken belief in their own unique ability to grasp the meaning of scripture, to form quite new religious views, which they wrongly think to be somehow the one original and correct set of beliefs. But non-traditionalism opens the door to liberal interpretations (interpretations that feel free, for what they feel to be good reasons, to rescind both traditions and specific scriptural commandments).

It seems, overall, that a commitment to Torah does not make for unanimity. On the contrary, it encourages a complex diversity, which seems to be an ineliminable feature of rabbinic Judaism. The slightly odd fact is that, although a study of Jewish religious history makes this quite obvious, a remarkable number of people spend their time denying it, and affirming that theirs is the only acceptable form of belief and practice. That, too, seems to be characteristic of many forms of religion, and it seems to arise from a refusal to distinguish between having a personal preference for one view and holding that everyone else ought to prefer it as well.

Truth and Freedom of Conscience

Religion is a matter of truth, and so it may seem obvious that if I believe what is true, other people ought to believe it also. But in fact what people ought to believe is related to more general conditions of knowledge, their other beliefs and so forth. What people ought to believe is what they think is true. That might be different from what is in fact true.

I ought to believe what I think is true. But all that follows about other people is that they ought to believe what they think is true. Perhaps we could say that ideally people ought to believe what is true. But morally they ought to believe what they think is true. Assuming they have taken all reasonable steps to think correctly, it must be the case that often, in ethics, in religion, in art, and in all issues of personal judgement, people often (morally) ought to believe different things, given the conditions of their knowledge. This is just to state that freedom to follow conscience is a morally good thing. It ought to be a first principle of religion, and it often is. But from it follows the principle that if I think a religious assertion is true, it does not follow that everyone else (morally) ought to agree with me. It does not even follow that I must *think* that everyone else ought to agree with me. From this in turn it follows that religious law cannot be imposed on others when they conscientiously do not believe it is binding on them. Particular communities of interpretation of law must be voluntaristic, freely accepted, and not compulsory.

Having said this, however, I am conscious that I have placed myself in opposition to some strict Orthodox viewpoints. Some Orthodox Jews believe that God's Law should be the Law for all Jews. All Jews should keep the Sabbath rules, the food laws, and all the other laws too, whether they feel like it or not. For these are laws given by God for the Jewish people, and they are conditions of being a member of the covenant people. It is not a matter of choice, any more than being born in a particular country, or of particular parents, is a choice. Thus arises the central problem of any system of religious law. Is the imposition of God's Law incompatible with moral autonomy, with personal choice of how one should live?

Problems with Revealed Law – an Argument for a Liberal View

If it was quite clear that there is a God who has given a set of unchangeable and universal moral laws that are conducive to human welfare, associated with eternal punishments and rewards for obedience, then it would undoubtedly be rational to obey such laws.

Unfortunately almost every detail of this supposition is highly controversial. First, it is not at all clear that there is a God. There are very powerful arguments against the existence of a benevolent creator. Many informed and intelligent people do not think that a personal God exists, and there are many Jews who are atheists. This means that many Jews do not want to live under a law whose only justification is that God gave it. There must be some other justification for law, in any society that contains a good number of atheists, or even agnostics.

Second, there are many competing claims about what set of laws God may have given. Judaism, Christianity, Islam, and various schools of Hinduism all offer rather different sets of 'divinely given' laws. So it is unclear which set is truly given by God. In a situation of such unclarity, it is not rational to impose just one set of laws on every member of a society.

Third, the form in which the laws are given makes it unclear whether the laws are changeless or not. In the Hebrew Bible, laws are given in particular historical contexts, and in the course of a complex historical narrative. Are these laws revisable, in view of differing historical circumstances, or new technological possibilities? Further, some of the laws (for example, the ritual of the red cow, in Numbers 19, which seems to incorporate primitive purification rites that belong to tribal societies) seem to be ancient traditions that are now obsolete or without meaning in modern nation states. Can such ancient laws be changed or ignored?

Fourth, it is not clear whether divine laws are to be universally imposed by government, or whether they are to be accepted only by particular groups of believers, who will live alongside others who do not accept those laws. Orthodox Jews are on the whole happy to accept such a restriction, but some may want the laws imposed universally.

Fifth, it is disputed whether all revealed laws are conducive to human welfare. Rules that advocate stoning to death, bodily mutilation, the subjugation of women, and rigorous use of capital punishment – all characteristic of many early human societies – strike many people as cruel and unusual in states where the welfare of all is taken into consideration.

And sixth, it is not at all clear that there are any rewards or punishments after death. More importantly, it is not clear that obeying laws just out of fear of punishment or hope of reward is a truly moral motivation. Maybe it is better to do good just for its own sake. If so, appeal to divine punishment may actually undermine the highest morality, rather than supporting it. It might be rational to obey divine laws under such conditions, but it might not be very moral, after all.

If religion was a purely theoretical matter, these considerations would leave most of us in a state of permanent, and continually fluctuating, indecision. But religious commitment is not a purely theoretical matter. It is a practical commitment to a way of life, centred on values that are felt to be objective and rooted in a supreme spiritual being or state. Worship, prayer and meditation are practices intended to lead one to conscious relationship or union with a spiritual reality of supreme value. If a practice leads to such a sense of union, religious commitment (faith) is confirmed subjectively. But the evaluation of what is truly worthwhile, and commitment to a discipline of prayer, are primary.

Theoretical considerations enter as part of an attempt to ensure that one's idea of the supreme reality is coherent. But they are not the necessary foundation of religious practice. You do not have to prove God exists before you can worship God. Worship comes first, but you do have to think the idea of God is possible and coherent. The existence of God is not theoretically certain, or even overwhelmingly probable. But it is presupposed to the practice of prayer and the postulate that some values are objective, and it should be probable enough to be the object of a fully rational belief. What this means is that we do not start from a theoretical certainty that there is a God who has given specific commands, and then simply list what those commands are. We start from participation in a specific community of prayer, and acceptance of its main values, and then proceed to theoretical belief in God.

It can be part of such a communities' internal beliefs that a set of commands has been given by God. What they are not justified in saying is that it is theoretically certain to all, whether in their community or not, that there is a God who has given these commands, and that therefore these commands have supreme authority for all.

Religious Law in a Multi-cultural World

Membership of the community and acceptance of its key values comes first. Humans are born into societies and receive their values and knowledge from their societies. But in a world in which there are many diverse societies it is a limitation of knowledge to insist that someone may not engage with other societies and learn from them. Where there is value-conflict between groups, it is a mark of rationality to know exactly what the conflict is, to try to understand why it exists, and to evaluate the conflict for oneself.

A religion exists to encourage and sustain practices, values and experiences of specific kinds. Where many religions exist, the seeker for truth should ideally have knowledge of them. Minimally, one should know that different practices, values, experiences and beliefs exist and are followed by people in good conscience and often with a theoretical basis that is more or less equal in probability to one's own. Beliefs about values and practices are not theoretically decidable, in the way that beliefs about physical facts are. If I say, 'God gave these commands to Moses', I have to accept that is not theoretically establishable. There is no way of reasonably ensuring universal assent to the belief. So I have to say: 'My tradition holds that . . . ' It is only probable (and many would hold, not very probable at that) that what my tradition holds is true. So I commit myself to accept what my tradition says, to put my trust in the tradition.

Why should I do that? I trust this tradition, because I trust its testimony to the occurrence of specific events in which God has been disclosed, because I think it is guided by God. And that is because I think God is genuinely known in this tradition, that a transfigured life is possible, apprehension of God is possible – that is, liberation from evil and unity with a being of supreme value is possible. It is the success of practice and the occurrence of transforming experience that makes trust rational. Two things seem to follow.

First, this is justifiable only for those who are engaged in this way of life. Second, exactly what is justified is subject to debate. For some, complete submission to authority without question is what is justified. For others, the submission to authority is justified only to the extent entailed or strongly suggested by the authenticity of the way of life. Religious law is valid only for those engaged in that religious life. And there will be internal disagreements possible between those who have to judge exactly how much authority engagement in the way of life licenses (for example, is a literal interpretation of Genesis licensed by trust in the authority of Orthodox Judaism? Or is such an interpretation too far removed from the possibility of liberating experience to be taken as a necessary part of the tradition?).

In religion, the practical has priority over the theoretical. So the problem arises: how much theoretical knowledge is required as a presupposition of the relevant practical commitment? A minimalist view is that we only need theoretical knowledge that is directly presupposed by the validity of liberating experience – for instance, that there is a supremely good reality (for example, God), that liberation is possible, that a way of liberation has been promulgated at some historic point by some historical person or persons, and such persons had a deeper insight into the nature of God, being liberated and having a deep experience of God themselves. A maximalist view would be that everything taught in the tradition – the literal truth of Genesis, for example – must be accepted. Between these extremes, there are many possibilities of belief. But perhaps the uniting strand behind all that diversity is acknowledgement that in this tradition a liberating and fulfilling apprehension of a supremely good reality is found. All theoretical beliefs should point towards this starting-point and goal of the religious life. This is a second principle of a liberal interpretation of religion. The first principle is that people conscientiously differ, and ought to follow their consciences – therefore religion cannot be imposed upon them. This is the principle of freedom of belief. The second is that the core of religious belief is liberating experience of the supreme Good, and that no religious disputes that imperil or diminish such experience are to be entertained. This is the principle of the primacy of the practical. It is a principle that is well expressed in the typical Jewish emphasis on practice rather than theoretical orthodoxy. But the practice is not just an external obedience to a set of rules. It is a practice of the total submission of heart and mind to God – the love of God with all one's heart and soul and might (Deut. 6.5). If this is firmly enshrined as the basic principle of religious faith, then the way is open to see that the question of which specific laws are to be literally obeyed is a subsidiary matter, upon which there will be conscientious disagreements, and that should always be answered by reference back to the basic principle.

In addition, any specific religious law will have to be proposed as the law for a specific community, membership of which is a matter for free personal assent. This may seem rather idealistic, in a world in which many people are strongly controlled by social custom. But it is a goal towards which a global interpretation of religious law should move, and one that is strongly implied by the principles of religious freedom and the primacy of liberative religious experience.

The Bible as a Record of Developing Perceptions of God

The Hebrew Scriptures give a record of developing perceptions of God, guided by God yet never entirely free of limiting cultural factors and beliefs. The statutes and ordinances of Torah and Talmud originate in diverse historical circumstances, and record many opinions addressed to specific situations. They do not present one systematic theological or legal treatise, but many different strands – for example, the Book of the Covenant (Ex. 20—23), the Holiness Code (Lev. 17—end) and the Ritual Decalogue (Ex. 34). These were bound together into an edited narrative of the patriarchs and the exodus. This internally complex structure of Torah may lead us to expect a continuing development of thought about how the covenant people are to act in relation to their God. Such development, we need to remember, is not necessarily from worse to better. There may be regressions of understanding as well as advances. But there is certainly change, and there does seem to be a deepening of the understanding of God in the writings of the greater prophets. The Mosaic Law lays down the guidelines, the originating covenant binding this people to God. But the Hebrew Bible continues as a narrative in which the greater prophets bring new insights and are even critical of many of the ritual requirements of Torah.

With the destruction of the second Temple, the whole structure of Torah, which had been centred on the Temple and priesthood, was changed dramatically. Now the *mitzvot* themselves became the central focus of Jewish life. Rabbinic Judaism was a complete rethinking of Jewish tradition. Torah becomes a way of relation to God, originating with Abraham and Moses and the prophets, but having its own dynamic as something that has changed dramatically in the past because of external circumstances, and so does not preclude radical change again.

Progressive Jews may hold that formulae like 'God said to Moses' are not to be taken literally, as though God spoke or wrote specific words. 'God spoke to me' is often used in a metaphorical sense, to mean that after due reflection I came to an opinion, which I hope and believe was prompted by God. In a similar way, the biblical accounts of Moses' meetings with God may be framed in metaphorical terms, which depict the gradual formation of a body of laws over quite a long period of time as if it was the giving of those laws to Moses all at once.

It seems that much biblical language is metaphorical – talk of God riding on the clouds or walking in a garden, for instance. So we might take the whole biblical narrative metaphorically, depicting the long development of a legal tradition, in which some laws become central and normative for Jewish tribal life, and others lose importance as Israel becomes a monarchy or a people in the diaspora. The Hebrew Bible in its diversity, its different styles and even different languages (Hebrew and Aramaic), and its frequent insistence upon the final mystery of the divine being, is fairly amenable to a more developmental and non-literal view of inspiration. This is true of both orthodox and liberal views. Both views – that God dictates Torah to Moses, and that Torah is a cumulative tradition of tribal law under God – are possible within Judaism. Which is accepted – and it is not an all-or-nothing choice – depends upon general views of how God interacts with the world, and in particular on how one thinks God influences the prophets (by dictation or by some more general form of inspiration). That issue is not decided by the text itself.

My personal view is that elements in Torah such as the idea of 'blood-guilt' lying on the land, or 'magical' rituals for removing impurity, show the influence of ancient tribal taboos that have been incorporated into a later monotheistic cult, but become irrelevant in the fully ethical monotheism that the later prophets taught. This would mean that God does not literally dictate the laws, but is consistent with a view that God 'inspires' or guides the process of law-gathering and interpretation, as it develops over the centuries.

Such a view would lead one to expect a continuing development in the interpretation of religious law. In practice, however, this might not differ radically from a more Orthodox or traditional view. For even when it is held that God dictated Torah, this Torah was given to a particular people at a particular time. Any set of laws that remains the same in radically changing circumstances comes to have a very different meaning. The crucial task for all lawyers is to discern, as well as they can, what principles underlay those specific rules for a very different culture, and how those principles can be most appropriately formulated in rules for today. There is much room here for personal judgement, and for a developing insight into the will of God, paradigmatically expressed in a set of statutes and ordinances for a tribal Bronze Age society, but always intended to provide the normative precedents for judicious decision-making in very different contexts.

If divine revelation is given in the form of laws, then one would expect the legal interpretation and application of these laws to play a central role in the discernment of the will of God. So even when an Orthodox Jew says, 'This is exactly what God dictated to Moses', there remains the question of how we are to understand that normative expression of God's will in a changed world and in changed social conditions. That is a lawyer's job. That is why the jurisprudential or rabbinic tradition is central to a Jewish view of scripture. That is why there will always be a central place in religious Judaism for diversity and for developing understandings of what the law requires. And that is why there may not always be as much disagreement over many social laws between progressive and conservative views as one might at first expect.

Secular and Religious Law – a Misleading Dichotomy?

I have posed the problem of religious law as the problem of how it can coexist with secular law. But there is no agreed 'secular law' or secular idea of justice that can be simply contrasted with religious law. Politics is a field of competing views, sometimes violently competing. Communists, socialists, liberals, conservatives, fascists, royalists, aristocrats, meritocrats and democrats, all have conflicting views about how human society should be organized, and such conflicts often lead to violence.

It is arguable – indeed it seems pretty clear – that the purely secular and indeed anti-religious laws of Marxist-Leninist communism led to more repression and violence in the twentieth century than any set of religious laws. We must not assume that secular laws will all be nicely liberal, while religious laws will be repressive and inhumane. In face of the dictatorships, both right-wing and left-wing, that disfigure so much of our globe, we find that repressive societies are not uncommon, whether they are religiously based or not. And we might well find that some of the major humanizing influences in our world have religious roots. So we should be wary of posing the problem as one of secular humanism versus religious repression. Very few political systems in our world are humane, measured by any standard. What about the fact that in a secular society laws are invented by people, and in Judaism the law is given by God? That sounds like a huge difference, but the facts are more complicated. There are versions of secular justice for which the important factor is respect for personhood, for the dignity and primary importance of human creative freedom and responsible decision-making. A just political system should seek to enhance the distinctive personal capacities of all human beings, and ensure that none are without the basic means of some such personal self-realization. That is, it could be said, the philosophy of secular humanism. It requires no religious sanction, and it will oppose any form of religious life that threatens to undermine human dignity, care for the weak, or the importance of the informed critical pursuit of truth, beauty and goodness.

I have argued, however, in my first chapter, that in fact the philosophy of humanism is best supported by a view that can make a place for objective obligation and for the unique moral importance of personal life (whether or not individuals recognize such obligation and importance). Humanism is sometimes seen as a liberation from old religious shackles. But I think it is rather a genuine inner development of religious faith. For it is the book of Genesis that depicts humans as created 'in the image of God' (Gen. 1.27). God is a creator of life and beauty, one who is supremely wise and just, one whose knowledge encompasses all things, and who is merciful and full of loving-kindness. So humans, created in this image, are most truly human when they are creative, wise, just, knowledgeable, merciful, kind and loving. A firm foundation for belief in the moral dignity of humans is belief that they are created in God's image, and a strong basis for moral obligations to other persons is that God has created us and them to grow together into the likeness of God.

If this is so, religious law and the concerns of humanism should not be opposed. Religion can give to humanism – the concern that human life should flourish – an objective foundation and goal. Humanism – the search for what does enable human life to flourish – can give to religion a major key to the interpretation and application of ancient religious laws. This might be called a third principle of religious liberalism, the principle of personalism. All our moral and social principles must ultimately be judged by their effectiveness in promoting universal human flourishing and welfare. This is not, in my view, a new anti-religious principle that frees morality from the tutelage of religious authority. It is a deeply religious principle that emerges from reflection on the central concerns of religious faith, and from a determination to express the prophetic concern for universal justice and mercy in ways consistent with our growing knowledge of the natural world, and with the great historical changes in culture that force ancient rules to be expressed and applied in new ways.

Moses said, 'Choose life so that you and your descendants may live, loving the Lord your God, obeying him, and holding fast to him, for that means life to you and length of days' (Deut. 30.19 and 20). Again, 'Now, O Israel, what does the Lord your God require of you? Only to fear the Lord your God, to walk in all his ways, to love him, to serve the Lord your God with all your heart and with all your soul, and to keep the commandments of the Lord your God and his decrees that I am commanding you today, for your own well-being' (Deut. 10.12 and 13). If religious law is for human well-being, it will not differ widely from secular law that aims at the same goal.

Problems with Religious Law

The fact is, however, that some interpretations of religious law do come into conflict with the principles of human flourishing. Religious laws are often seen as repressive and archaic, as the arbitrary commands of a tyrannical God rather than as the rules given by a loving and rational God for human well-being. Perhaps the first thing to establish, then, is that God is not a tyrant, and religious laws are not meant to be arbitrary or repressive.

There can be no meaningful moral conversation with those who think God is a tyrant who can command anything God wants, without reference to moral or rational considerations. Our conversation can only be with those who initially agree that God is good (and will therefore not command anything immoral) and wise (and will therefore not command anything irrational). But there can be little doubt that the main Jewish traditions unequivocally teach the existence of a good and wise God. If this is agreed, the problem is to discern which religious laws seem not to advocate universal human flourishing. Then we must decide how they might be interpreted in ways consistent with their main underlying intention that human life should flourish.

We must not forget, of course, that human flourishing, from a Jewish viewpoint, must lie in achieving the ultimate goal of human life, the knowledge and love of the God of Abraham, Isaac and Jacob, whose will was revealed to Moses and the Hebrew prophets. But, while this may add significant elements to a secular view of human welfare, we would not expect the way to such a goal to conflict radically with what can be seen to be conducive to human flourishing in more secular contexts.

In Judaism, possible sources of conflict with a generally humanist morality lie mainly in the biblical promise of an *eretz* Israel from the Nile to the Euphrates (Gen. 15.18); the death penalty for apostasy and for various sexual offences, including homosexuality; rules concerning slavery; the killing of animals without first stunning them; and various prohibitions concerning women and their social role.

First, with regard to the promise of the land and the rules for conquest, it is as well to remember that these are rules for a Bronze Age nomadic tribal people in search of a homeland. If they were taken as unchangeable and irrevocable laws, they would provide a recipe for endless war in the Middle East.

There is already enough violence in the Middle East, but it is not all religiously based. Israel is a secular state, and most Zionists were not religious believers. The Israeli government has no plans for annexing Syria and Jordan, and their concern is to live as a nation in security, in borders largely established by Britain and the major powers in 1947. Orthodox rabbis may or may not be pleased by the existence of the state of Israel – some believe that eretz Israel should not exist until the Messiah comes, and disapprove of the present state. But virtually all the Orthodox regard the promise of the land as associated with God's warning that the land would be lost by disobedience, which it was. The land will not be returned until the Messianic age, which is perhaps beyond foreseeable history or political intrigue. Thus these rules, like those concerning slavery and those concerning the Temple and its sacrifical rituals, are obsolete, belonging to a past age before the monarchy, the exile and the diaspora. These laws were for a time when, according to Torah itself, Israel was wholly obedient to God. That time is long past and will not return until the Messiah comes. And when that happens, they will in any case be rendered obsolete by the reign of peace and justice that he will bring.

There is always the possibility that some Jews may agitate for the rebuilding of the Temple on its old site, where the Muslim Dome of the Rock now stands. That would be a major and catastrophic act of aggression. But it is important to be clear that rabbinic Judaism has renounced the Temple law and the Levitical priesthood. Joshua ben Hananiah, around 100 CE, formally declared that the 'seven nations' of Canaan are no longer identifiable, thus rendering all laws concerning the conquest of Canaan obsolete. In that sense, rabbinic Judaism is inherently revisionist. It is committed to the belief that some religious laws are to be revised or abandoned, because of circumstances. Possibly these circumstances were envisaged in the Torah itself, as it set the blessings and curses of God before the Israelites. That is partly why conservative Judaism looks primarily to the Talmud, seeing it as a source of precedents for new legal decisions. Such decisions may be conservative or more radical, but either way the emphasis has moved from literal obedience to a written text to trying to decide what God's will is now, using as precedents laws that applied to a very different culture and historical epoch.

Seen in that light, liberal or progressive Judaism is not a quite different phenomenon from Orthodox Judaism. It just stands towards one end of the spectrum of possible legal decision-making that is present in all mainstream Judaism. There is not, after all, a huge gulf between saying that God gave the *mitzvot*, but rabbis have to decide if and how they apply in very different situations, and saying that the *mitzvot* are early human attempts to discern the will of God for the people of Israel, and that such attempts must continue in a very different world. In both cases, the way is open to accept that things change, that new cases require new legal decisions, but that ancient precedents, both in Bible and Talmud, trace the development of a distinctive legal tradition in a way it is important to know and understand.

Second, in the light of this discussion, it is not hard to see how the use of capital or severe physical punishments in Torah has been modified in rabbinic discussion. It has increasingly come to be seen that killing people is not the most humane way of 'loving your neighbour as yourself', and that mercy may radically modify the strict demands of purely retributive justice. Strict punitive justice encourages intolerance, prejudice and moral censoriousness, as well as raising the danger of killing in error those who are innocent. Torah holds that rebellious or drunken sons, or those who place a curse on their parents, can be stoned (Deut. 21). Murderers must be put to death (Num. 35), and executed by the next of kin of the victim, otherwise 'blood-guilt' lies upon the land.

If we have any sense of history, we will see that the insistence upon a 'tit for tat' punishment is more merciful than some other punishments common in human societies in the late Bronze Age. Torah distinguishes between murder and manslaughter, and provides for 'cities of refuge' where those who have caused death without malicious intent will be safe from vengeance. But conditions in a tribal society are very different from those in a modern nation, and it has become possible to find other ways of dealing with murder.

The basic principle of revision is that punishment should ideally provide the possibility of repentance and reform – a possibility that execution cannot give. There is scope for revising ancient laws in accordance with the deeper principle that all (human) life should be respected, as created in God's image.

The doctrine of revision is of the greatest importance, when considering what religious law requires. An Orthodox interpretation would say that each law enshrines some important principle. It exists for a reason. It remains an important principle that sons should not be rebellious, that one should not commit adultery, commit apostasy or practice witchcraft. Yet we need to qualify even these statements further, for what constitutes apostasy or witchcraft needs to be specified more closely. We might say that it is not immoral for a Jew to convert to another faith, but it is immoral for a Jew to turn from God out of a desire for pleasure or material success. Or we could say that it is not immoral to be a pagan, and use herbs to heal people, but it is immoral to place spells on people to try to harm them.

We need to ask what it was that the command was really identifying as wrong, and for this we need to use the sorts of definitional procedures that are common in all legal systems. In other words, judges need to interpret the law. Different interpretations are possible, and definitions of exactly what is wrong about apostasy, for example, may get increasingly complex. In the Talmud there are many examples of rabbinic differences of interpretation, and discussion of difficult cases is an important part of Talmudic education.

Religious law requires complex judicial procedures, framing new interpretations and setting various relevant precedents alongside one another. Judicial wisdom is required in deciding what precedents are relevant, and in deciding which commands may override or abrogate others. There is much room for diversity and flexibility in such a system of religious law. Whether such flexibility exists or not will largely depend upon social circumstances and the general temperaments of the interpreters – the rabbis – in specific societies. It may vary from place to place, and it does.

In general, there are some commands at a high level of generality that are usually thought to govern the interpretation of more particular commands. We would not go far wrong if we thought that 'Love the Lord your God with all your heart and soul and might' (Deut. 6) and 'You shall love your neighbour as yourself' (Lev. 19) were the most general principles for governing particular decisions about religious law. For an observant Jew they would not replace all the more specific laws about food and religious observance, but they would lead, and they have led, to abandonment of stoning to death, as something which it is increasingly difficult to see as exhibiting neighbour-love. There is room for dispute here, and some would still see capital punishment as required by law (though few would literally ask for 'an eye for an eye'). But it is possible to be an Orthodox Jew and abandon capital punishment, where there are other forms of punishment available, that may offer some hope of reformation and repentance for the offender, and may not require the taking of human life.

Such disputes rarely turn on the simple assertion that 'it is in the Torah, so we have to do it'. They can hardly do so, when stoning to death and burning have been abandoned. They reflect more general views, whether religiously based or not, on what punishment is suitable for a murderer. Insofar as a religious belief leads one to think of God as compassionate and merciful – and thus as a model for compassionate and merciful human behaviour – and to think of human life as of infinite or at least very great value, there will be a religious argument against capital punishment.

The dispute is between rigorist disciplinarians and humane optimists about human nature. Such oppositions of temperament exist both within and without religion, and both can find resources in scripture if they wish to do so. It is not the case that religious law is, as such, more rigorist than secular law. There will always be rigorists in religion. In Judaism, they will revel in their separateness and distinctness. But there will be diversity even among rigorists, since they will interpret the law in different ways, putting emphasis on different parts of it, and applying it to new circumstances in different ways.

One thing, however, should be unequivocally clear. There is no place for hatred, vengefulness, desire for domination or suppression of others among religious rigorists. Such things are condemned at the deepest level by Torah's insistence on loving-kindness, benevolence, justice and mercy. Moreover, rigorism is not by any means the only religious option. Many who see diversity and development and even radical change (as with the ending of the Temple sacrifices) as central to Jewish practice over the years, will see Torah as inherently humane and flexible, a set of underlying principles to be discerned with practical wisdom rather than a set of changeless rules which simply have to be applied. They will tend to see the discussions and decisions recorded in the Talmud as opinions for a specific occasion or for a specific group of people. Opinions can change with circumstances, and they can become more sensitive over time. What is needed at one time is not necessarily what is needed at another. If this is so, the application of religious law will be in constant dialogue with the wider society in which it is set.

I have distinguished three senses of religious liberalism – the principle of freedom of belief, the principle of the primacy of the practical, and the principle of personalism. To this a fourth principle might now be added, a preparedness to revise one's opinions if that seems to be required by advances in knowledge or radical changes in the social conditions of existence. This might be called a principle of critical belief – not that one is to criticize everything in a negative way, but that one is prepared to subject one's beliefs to critical scrutiny when new knowledge makes that necessary.

Liberal Judaism upholds all these principles. They might even be said to be the constitutive principles of liberal Judaism. But it is important to note that religious conservatives and traditionalists can also accept these principles, even though they may not make them the only or the definitive principles of their faith. The freedom to practice one's faith, the primacy of practical commitment over doctrinal agreement, the importance of using one's God-given talents to the full, and the encouragement of critical debate and discussion – these are all central features of the Jewish faith. In this sense, even the most conservative Jew is liberal. It is paradoxical but not surprising that liberalism in religion springs from, yet is always in creative tension with, the conservative tradition of Jewish religious law.

Third, among rules concerning sex in Torah, if a priest's daughter becomes a prostitute, she shall be burned (Lev. 21). Having more than one wife, and the possession of concubines, is allowed, though kings should not have 'many wives' (Deut. 17), lest they turn from God. Priests may not marry a divorcee, though otherwise such marriages are not prohibited (Lev. 21). Men and women should not exchange clothing (Deut. 22). Dissimilar things should not be mixed – like ploughing with an ox and an ass, wearing linen and wool, or sowing with two kinds of seed (Lev. 19). Women who claim to be virgins when they marry but are not may be stoned (Deut. 22), as may those who commit adultery. Rape carries a fine of 50 pieces of silver and life-long marriage to the victim (Exod. 22). Men may divorce women for 'indecency' (very widely defined), but may not remarry a wife they have divorced (Deut. 24). Those who have intercourse with other men or with animals must die (Lev. 20). Men should marry a dead brother's wife to provide a son for her, if she had no son (Deut. 25).

There has been development in mitigating punishments for these offences, in an increasing preference for monogamy, in the ending of Levirate marriage (marrying your deceased brother's wife), and in revising the rules for divorce (permitting women to divorce men, and in general giving women greater equality). The issue of homosexual practice is still controversial. But looking at the context of these laws, three main themes seem to predominate. One is an ancient taboo on not mixing dissimilar things, or confusing categories. Cross-dressing or same-sex intercourse violate this taboo. To the extent we now regard taboos as obsolete, that is no longer a relevant consideration.

A second consideration is that sexual practices merely for self-gratification or performed in fertility rites are considered improper. That is true both of heterosexual and homosexual practices, and reflects an interest that sexual relations should take place in the context of a long-term personal relationship of fidelity and trust. It is probable that practices of pederasty and promiscuous sex were associated with homosexuality. Long-term same-sex unions are in a different category, one that the laws do not envisage.

Furthermore, there is concern for the propagation of children in a stable family. It is unlikely that same-sex partnerships would undermine this concern, and so we might say that greater knowledge of the genetic basis of sexual preference would not countermand the ban on sexual promiscuity, but might encourage the view that same-sex relations should be permitted, if they are primarily based on personal love, trust and fidelity.

Fourth, Torah is not an obvious text-book for good inter-faith relations. All the sacred sites of the Canaanites were to be destroyed (Deut. 12). Prophets tempting Israelites to worship other gods were to be killed. Apostates, mediums and witches were to be stoned to death (Deut.13). These are perhaps the most difficult laws of all for a secularist to understand. It needs to be borne in mind that the worship of God was not just a matter of an optional belief in a supernatural being. It was bound up with acceptance of the whole Torah as a way of life. 'Canaanite worship' was identified with cultic prostitution, orgiastic fertility rites, the sacrifice of children to the gods, attempts to use spirit powers to curse others, the worship of wealth and power, and with a divorce of religious practice from moral laws of justice and benevolence.

Deviations from Torah were seen as treason, as undermining the basic values of Israelite society. God had called the Israelites to a special vocation of proclaiming a God of justice and mercy to the world, and to reject that calling was to exclude oneself from the covenant community. Perhaps the nearest analogy for a secularist would be that someone who calls for and works actively for the overthrow of a state, secular or otherwise, cannot be tolerated. Many secular (communist) governments have killed thousands, even millions, of people for such crimes. Many in more liberal societies would at least call for their banning, exile or imprisonment. It is not at all obvious how far a community, especially a relatively small one under constant threat from hostile neighbours, can peacefully tolerate the existence of deeply subversive elements.

Today Orthodox Jews do not call for Jewish converts to Islam or Christianity to be killed. Freedom of religious practice has been a hard-won value. What it requires is acceptance that other belief-systems are not all morally subversive or harmful to human welfare. It requires acceptance that religious commitment should be voluntary, since religious beliefs are not just social conventions, but make truth-claims that are legitimately contested, and are not theoretically establishable with certainty. And it requires acceptance that there can be, and perhaps even that there needs to be, a proper area of conflicting beliefs, of a plurality of interpretations and world-views, within a coherent and just society.

An Orthodox Jew today can say that these laws were given by God for an emergency situation in the history of Israel, whose conditions are long past. More radically, one can see these laws as expressing a limited and imperfect perception of what God wills for a community wholly devoted to obedience to a divine moral purpose, a will that was perceived more clearly later in the history of Israel's search to discern the divine will. More radically still, these laws can be seen as fairly typical of the primitive moral rules from that historical epoch, that permit the legitimized expression of violence and hatred. A morality of greater compassion and sensitivity will rescind them, and this was done later in rabbinic tradition. Theoretically diverse, all these views nevertheless agree that no one should seek literal application of the laws today, and that what they require is a more sensitive understanding of non-Jewish religious beliefs, and a more compassionate attitude to the treatment of offenders. Both these things are central to Torah, in the requirement that all are to be treated with concern for their welfare, which entails that one should seek to understand why they are as they are.

Fifth, rituals for purification (Lev. 14, Deut. 21 and Num. 19) are obsolete, as are all the rules for the sacrificial cult and the priesthood. Rules concerning the need for purification after menstruation and after childbirth (33 days for a boy; 66 days for a girl: Lev.12) are often retained by Orthodox rabbis. But in principle such rules are as subject to revision as rules concerning skin-diseases and rites for their purification.

The same holds true for rules about contact with the dead. A conservative application of this rule makes post-mortem examinations and pathology impossible. But there can easily be a rabbinic argument that under special conditions, contact with the dead serves the purposes of life and of justice, and is then justified. Which interpretation is adopted is partly determined by how bound to particular ancient precedents rabbis feel, and by the authority given in practice to their judgements. Since rabbinic tradition accepts that Jews are not bound to literal interpretations of Torah, there is room for disagreement on interpretation. Traditionalist views will place great store by ancient or near universal precedents. Reforming views will rather emphasize new knowledge or changed circumstances in forming an interpretation.

Positive Aspects of Religious Law

I may seem to have concentrated on the negative aspects of religious law, those that cause difficulties for modern moral sensibilities. But the Torah contains many positive features, which are the real foundation for Jewish love of God's Law: 'I have taken your law as my heritage for ever; for it is the joy of my heart' (Ps. 119). It is because the Law shows the way to live fully in a conscious relationship of love for God, that it is the joy of the heart.

First, the rules for tithing are a reminder that all things are given by God, that we cannot use material goods just for selfish purposes. Tithed animals must be eaten at a feast, in which foreigners, orphans and widows are to share (Deut. 14). So the worship of God is connected with feasting and enjoyment, and with concern for those who are less fortunate. The literal form of these rules became obsolete with the ending of sacrifices, but the underlying principles of fellowship and benevolence remain important. Rules governing religious festivals have been radically changed with the destruction of the Temple and priesthood. But the major festivals are still celebrated, though without sacrifices. On the Sabbath, work, travel and the lighting of fires is forbidden. At Pesech (Passover), the exodus from Egypt is remembered. The three great festivals of Mazzoth (unleavened bread), Pentecost (wheat harvest) and Succoth (tabernacles) are built around the barley, wheat and fruit harvests of the ancient agricultural year, reinterpreted as commemorations of the liberation of Israel from slavery, the giving of the Torah by Moses, and the time of living in tents in the wilderness.

The emphasis is on thanksgiving for liberation from the slavery of sin, on trust in God, on repentance for wrong-doing, on family celebration, and on sharing with the poor. Yom Kippur, the Day of Atonement, expresses total dependence on God, and the desire to lay aside all that separates people from God. The rite of sending a goat into the wilderness has been dropped, and Yom Kippur is now generally regarded as a day for remembering one's sins against justice and compassion, and asking God's forgiveness.

In the Torah, it was only ritual or unintentional offences that were forgiven. Sacrifice for presumptuous sin was not thus forgiven, but was to be punished (Num. 15.30). It is common today, however, to ask forgiveness also for sins that have been committed intentionally. The great positive emphasis of these laws is on thanksgiving for the good things of life, enjoyment of them, and sharing with those who are less fortunate.

Second, the ritual purity laws, while again mostly superseded by medical advances, have two main functions. In the case of food laws, they serve to set apart the Jews by making every meal a remembrance of the covenant. Then there are laws concerning bodily wholeness and health (with leprosy, bodily discharges and contact with the dead). While the specific content of these laws may change, the underlying concern for the celebration of life and health is a characteristically Jewish emphasis on the goodness of physical bodily existence. Judaism is not at all an other-worldly religion. It celebrates life, and one might say that the Torah exists to point the way to greater life and health for both individuals and the community.

Third, according to Torah, every seven years land shall lie fallow, and the poor may eat whatever grows there (Exod. 23). All debts to fellow Israelites shall be cancelled, and all Hebrew slaves freed and given liberal provisions (Deut. 15). Every fiftieth year, at the Year of Jubilee (the name is derived from the Hebrew for 'ram', referring to the ram's horn that was to be sounded at this time), all property shall be returned to its original owner.

It is doubtful whether these laws were ever applied literally, but they clearly express principles of practical concern for the poor, the undesirability of slavery, and the evil of accumulating great wealth and property. The chief moral principles they suggest are that ideally all people should be free, and that all wealth belongs to God, and must be used in the service of God and for the welfare of God's creation.

Few, if any, rabbis would seek to apply the rules concerning release from slavery, which presuppose that such an institution exists (Hebrews are permitted to possess foreign slaves), in a literal sense. Social institutions have in this respect progressed, and in a direction at least hinted at in the Jubilee laws. The lesson is that we must always seek the deeper principles that underlie specific context-dependent rules, and discern principles that reflect the highest moral insights of Torah, insights which may only be hinted at in some of its specific laws.

It is as well to remember, however, that 'slavery' can be taken to cover any degrading or unduly onerous employment. In that sense, many forms of slavery still exist in our world. If we are to see all people as created in God's image, we should reverence each individual as a reflection or partial expression of God. This is incompatible with all forms of slavery, and it is a religious obligation to see, so far as is possible, that no one on earth is deprived of the opportunity to live in freedom from oppression and in economic security.

Fourth, Torah insists that judges should be just and impartial (Deut. 16). Kings or rulers are not to consider themselves greater than others, and are to fear God; their power is not absolute (Deut. 17). While the punishments of Torah are severe, there is an important provision that people cannot be charged on the evidence of only one witness, and that false witnesses shall receive the punishment that the accused would have received (Deut. 19). The 'law of retaliation' forbids excessive punishments. Each person must be punished only for their own wrong-doing. Foreigners, widows and orphans are to be treated justly and equitably. Those on trial for their lives should be helped wherever possible. Vengeance, dishonesty, promise-breaking, exploitation, malice, bribery, stealing, cheating, lying and cursing are all condemned.

The one great insight of religious law, that more than balances all the disadvantages of literal interpretations of ancient rules, is that the rule of justice is other than the rule of human beings. Whatever the positive laws of nations may be, there is one objective law of justice, that all people are responsible agents who must be respected impartially for their humanity alone, and not for their social position. In this insight lies the foundation for a belief in inalienable human rights. We owe to each person a duty to preserve them in life, to allow them the freedom to pursue their own projects responsibly, and to enable them to find some measure of fulfilment and happiness. For God has created them to live, to act freely, to realize their God-given capacities, and to be happy. What God has given, no human being should seek to take away.

Fifth, there are, finally, a number of laws encouraging benevolence to the poor. Lending at interest to those Israelites who are poor is prohibited (Deut. 23). People are allowed to eat grapes or wheat from the fields of others, but not to take them away in containers. Fields must not be reaped to the borders, and what is left is for the poor. Debtors must not be deprived of what they need to live (Deut. 24). The poor must be given sufficient for their needs (Deut. 15). The elderly must be respected. The Book of Leviticus commands that 'You shall love not only neighbours but also foreigners as you love yourself' (Lev. 19).

This final command, which is in fact part of the command to love the Lord God with heart, soul and strength (Deut. 6), sums up all the others, and provides the guiding principle for interpreting the whole of Torah, as a living, dynamic principle of relationship to a God who is known as the liberator and ruler of the covenant community. It is not only the strict rules of justice that are to be pursued, but also the open-hearted principles of kindness and care for the disadvantaged. How could we fail to be kind when all that we are and have is a gift from God, and a gift that is given so that we may share with others the generosity of God? Therefore, together with the love of God, who is benevolent and kind, benevolence and loving-kindness to all are the most basic principles of Torah. It is by reference to those basic principles that religious law should always be interpreted.

Conclusion: a Humane Religious Law

Interpretations of religious law are diverse. Torah can be taken literally – which may produce conflicts with liberal laws of justice. But even then it is normally interpreted by rabbinic decisions. They are themselves diverse, and range from the more conservative (wishing to follow old established rabbinic decisions rather closely) to the more reforming (being prepared to let new conditions produce new legal applications). Thus there is no monolithic body of unchanging laws, and the way is always open to discussion and revision for adequate reason.

Liberal interpretations of Torah see it, not as literally dictated by God, but as made up of developing parts of a growing communal tradition, which may indeed be God-inspired. Torah can still have great importance as a sign of Jewish identity and covenant with God, but its particular rules will be more readily modified in accordance with the great and foundational principles of divine and human love.

For both conservatives and liberals, the heart of Torah is love of God and of God's creation. Torah is framed in terms of regulations given in specific historical contexts, partly the context of early settlement in a newly conquered territory. That context has changed considerably, and so rabbinic Judaism has needed continually to study Torah in order to find appropriate applications of its deepest principles in new circumstances.

There is not one agreed set of applications. A range of applications, varying from very traditionalist to radically reforming, exists. What is agreed, however, is that in Torah one finds the record of the attempts of a community to discern God's will for wholeness, justice and loving-kindness in the human world. These attempts are seen as responses to God's initiative in revealing the divine will.

Secular law and secular ideas of justice are at least as diverse as these interpretations of religious law. At one extreme is the Machiavellian and Hobbesian commendation of absolutist rule by the state. Then one has Burke's traditionalism, relying on established custom and abhorrent of radical change. Or there is Jeremy Bentham's liberalism, with minimal state activity, and freedom restricted only by the causation of clear physical harm to others. And there are many combinations in between. There are no secular ideas of justice as such.

The Enlightenment sought to formulate ideas of 'the rights of man', based on what reason would decree impartially for all. Reason was seen as the solvent of tradition, with its inbuilt inequalities based on the power of the few. In this social struggle, 'reason' was in fact a tool for claiming equality and freedom from oppression for the masses. It was, especially in France, seen as opposed to established religion, which was implicated in the *ancien régime* of absolutist monarchy. Yet the appeal to 'universal Reason' and the rights of the poor was itself rooted in religious ideas of God as the universal Reason (more commonly called *chokmah*, Wisdom), concerned for the welfare of all human beings, and especially for the poor.

Within religion itself, the broadening of concern to all humans and not just to one group was a struggle, but one that had been foreshadowed in Judaism by the acceptance that God cared for the whole earth, not just the people of Israel. And the idea that God was reasonable had to be disentangled from the alternative, more primitive, idea of an arbitrary commander the purpose of whose laws could not be fathomed by reason.

There is thus an internal religious critique, by which concern only for one faith or ethnic group is replaced by universal benevolence. And religious laws were gradually seen to stand in need of some justification in terms of human welfare. For the religious, such welfare ultimately involved relation to God, but the thought could not be sustained that one should just do whatever God was alleged to have said, whether it seemed right or not. If God is truly good, and if good is rationally desirable, then there should be some discernible relation between divine commands and rational human desires. It must therefore always be asked of a proposed divine law how it makes for human well-being and for a deepened relationship with a God of justice and compassion.

Within religion, there is a view of God that privileges one group (believers? Jews? Muslims? Christians?) above others, and that sees divine commands as beyond rational criticism. This is in conflict with a religious view of God who desires universal well-being, and whose commands can reasonably be seen to make for such well-being, given the presupposition that union with God's wisdom, love and bliss (the supernatural destiny of humanity) is the greatest good. The struggle between these ideas of God is a struggle for religious enlightenment, and it parallels the political struggle for greater justice and a more reasonable ordering of society.

Within secular society there is a view that one's own nation takes precedence over others, and that this nation must at any cost win the struggle for power that characterizes human existence. This is in conflict with the view that the good of all humanity is morally primary, and that reason requires that all should be roughly equal in freedom and opportunity.

The primitive moral view in religion is one where a non-rational God, not subject to moral criticism, simply legitimates the acts of one ethnic or national group in their ruthless struggle for power. The primitive view in secular law is where a ruthless human dictator pursues the interests of one nation or race at any cost to all others.

The enlightened view in religion is one in which a rational and benevolent God supports a striving for universal well-being, justice and benevolence. In secular law it is in which a rational and humane government seeks the well-being of all nations and especially of the poor and disadvantaged. Regrettably, a truly enlightened view is rarely realized on earth. But it should be clear that the greatest conflicts of belief are not between religious and secular justice, but between views that place reason and morality (the pursuit of the rationally desirable for all, considered impartially) high on either the religious or the secular agendas, and views that ignore reason and moral considerations (in the name either of national or of religious self-interest).

There is a secular basis for justice, in the pursuit of universal human welfare. Some religious views undermine such a pursuit, by caring only for the good of one group, and by valuing power (viewed as obedience to a God of absolute power) over compassion. Some secular views undermine it in precisely the same way, except that God does not figure in the equation.

For a secularist, universal human welfare must simply stand as a good, intuited as such and pursued for its own sake. A believing Jew should fully affirm this. But a Jew can add that obedience to the laws of justice is rooted in love of the creator who desires that all creatures should find fulfilment, who gives every human being a unique value and unique potentialities to realize, who helps those who seek such realization, and who will ultimately bring creation to fulfilment and final liberation from all that impedes fulfilment – that, is from evil. There is implicit here an ideal of justice, but it is not one that is in conflict with a humane secular ideal. It is rooted in the belief that all individuals are of worth, and that human society should enable all to realize something of that worth in their lives. Torah is the will of God for universal human fulfilment, and it expresses the specific calling of the Jews to be the mediators of this fulfilment to the world at large. It is the vision of God as universal creator, liberator and fulfiller of life that provides the key to interpreting religious law. Judaism, through the prophets, has given to the world the insight that religion is essentially concerned with moral action, with active love of the

Good. It has given to morality a transcendent dimension, making the vision of the Good the ultimate object of human love and desire, and union with the Good the ultimate goal of human striving. It is in such a vision that, in my view, religion and morality find their true relationship and their deepest significance.

Conclusion

I began this book by affirming that morality is autonomous in this sense: that the main moral principles of right and wrong, good and bad, are knowable by reason to all people, without the aid of revelation. But the really important question about morality is the question of its true nature. Is it a matter of human decision-making in a morally indifferent universe? Or is value somehow built into the universe itself, as an objective reality that can be apprehended by humans, and that plays a causal role in the very structure of the universe?

Religious views differ in many important ways. But most of them are united in affirming the objective existence of a being or state of supreme goodness, and in seeing the deepest purpose of human life as being the apprehension of this reality, and the mediation of eternal Goodness in the transitory events of time. For such religious views, morality is a path to the apprehension of supreme Goodness, and an attempt to conform human existence to it, so far as may be possible in a world corrupted by self-centred desire.

In the first chapter I showed how evolutionary biology can give an illuminating account of the origins of human morality. But it is, or should be, agnostic about whether God, the supreme Good, exists, is the true object of human moral awareness, and can ensure the final triumph of the good in the world. There is a non-religious morality. Religion does not undermine it. On the contrary, religion strengthens it by adding the strongest possible motivation – the love of God, the supremely good and beautiful – to moral endeavour, by giving reason to act for the sake of good alone, even when that demands the sacrifice of one's own life, and by affirming a hope for the triumph of goodness in a world that sometimes seems almost overwhelmed by evil. In this way, religion can transform morality, making it a sign of moral transcendence in a world of mundane desire, and making the pursuit of goodness the deepest motivation of a truly human life.

In subsequent chapters I traced out some consequences of such a religious view of morality by considering specific moral problems in the modern world, showing how different religions address them, and showing how there are intrinsic religious resources for finding personalist solutions to them.

I first considered issues of violence and warfare. Some people accuse religion of contributing to violence, and in the modern world Islam is often the object of such accusations. Of course Islam can be corrupted by hatred and desire, as can all religions and ethical and political systems in human life. But the Qur'an clearly places limits on resort to violence. Its doctrine of jihad is primarily a doctrine of striving for moral excellence and for submission to a God of mercy and compassion. And it sees warfare as a defence of justice for the oppressed, in opposition to hatred, cruelty and the aggressive lust for power.

The teaching of Islam is that there is, in the last resort, a place for the use of force in defending the innocent. But there is also always a place for mercy, and the goal must always be the restoration of a just and compassionate peace. Any attempt to impose beliefs by the sword is forbidden, as are attacks on the innocent, vindictiveness against the guilty, attempts to extend imperial power and hatred of any part of God's creation. The abuses of religion are many, and religions desperately need to identify and extirpate the ideologies of hatred and intolerance that are their characteristic vices. But religions ought to, and at their best they do, reinforce the demands of justice and compassion that are the only justifications for the use of force.

In the third chapter I considered the new moral problems raised by our ability to engineer the genetic codes of living beings.

Concentrating on the Christian tradition of a 'natural moral law', I suggested that Christians must see nature as having been created by God for a purpose. The evolutionary perspective of modern science is consistent with such a belief, and implies that humans may have a creative role to play in the realization of God's purpose for the universe. Christians should oppose any ethic that seeks to eliminate the weak in favour of the survival of the strong. That is not and cannot be God's purpose for the cosmos. But Christians should seek to extend capacities for personal flourishing – which include the virtues of cognitive understanding, creativity, compassion and communal responsibility. So a natural law morality for today will not simply leave the physical processes of nature alone. It will seek to eliminate all that frustrates personal flourishing, and use biotechnology, where appropriate, to extend and enrich the quality of personal life. It will justify reverence for the natural world as God's chosen and cherished creation, but will emphasize the duty of shaping that world to make it a fuller expression of the beauty and wisdom of the creator.

In the fourth chapter I considered a major area where natural law thinking has been traditionally used to justify the view that all sexual activity must be confined to marriage. Issues of gender and sexuality have become major areas of moral dispute in the modern world, among both religious and secular groups. I argued that if we subordinate physical to personal considerations, many traditional arguments are considerably weakened. In addition, consideration of the use of the Bible in morality points to the necessity of eschewing a literal application of specific biblical rules, which are mostly culture and context dependent, to very different modern situations. However, the underlying biblical principles of loyalty, fidelity, and the practice of sex as an expression of personal character and mutual love, does entail a sexual morality that strengthens long-term commitments of love. That, in my view, would permit same-sex loving unions, but it would disallow all forms of promiscuity and the disconnection of sexuality from the principle of committed love.

This is a much disputed topic, and my view may be a minority one among religions at present. If morality is truly autonomous, however, and if there are good reasons for revising traditional moral views in the modern world (because of a greater understanding of the biological and psychological bases of same-sex love, for instance), then those reasons will apply to religious morality too.

This leads me to say that the moral input of religion should not be in the promulgation of specific rules on the basis of revelation. Such specific rules may and do change in response to new knowledge and understanding. The relevant religious principle will be the primacy of the personal, which encourages a continuing search for all that makes for the flourishing of personal life. In a Christian context, this will be a search for what really makes for love of neighbour, of whatever race or gender, as oneself, and for love of God as the supremely personal – creative, sensitive and compassionate – embodiment of goodness. That, I think, is what a truly biblical morality is. It is in that context that sexual morality should be seen, and by that principle that all the specific moral rules of any Scripture should be judged.

Just as modern social and technological change has given rise to new moral disputes in the area of gender and sexuality, so it has generated new moral problems with regard to the beginning and end of life. In discussing those issues, in Chapter 5 I took Buddhism as a non-theistic faith that places reverence for life high on its agenda. I argued that new medical knowledge and techniques mean that the moral principles of compassion and concern for human welfare may conflict with the principles of respect for life as such. There is no easy resolution of such problems. My suggestion was that religious morality is primarily concerned with the development of inner attitudes or virtues of mind and heart, rather than with specific moral rules. Buddhists are bound both to respect and to have compassion for all sentient beings. That is an important reinforcement of morality, but it does not resolve conscientious disputes about what it is right to do in particular cases.

As I have argued that the provision of specific moral rules is not the distinctive task of religion, I turned finally in Chapter 6 to Judaism as a religion that does claim to have a divinely revealed law. I suggested that in fact there is no simple division between secular and religious law, and that the rabbinic interpretations of the law are both diverse and have changed considerably over time (especially after the destruction of the second Temple). The Torah marks out a distinctive path of relation to God, a path that does not conflict with universal moral principles and that is binding in its details only on a specific religious community.

Positively, the Torah provides a transcendent dimension to a more universal morality that is primarily concerned, as all humane morality is, with human flourishing. But conceptions of transcendence, like conceptions of morality, change and develop, and the law is not like a set of regulations that anyone can just read and apply. It is more like a set of normative precedents expressing underlying principles whose full force needs to be progressively apprehended by the community, and which are to be applied with discernment, wisdom and compassion. Religious law is not a set of unchangeable ancient rules. It is concerned with formulating and applying principles of justice and compassion in a rapidly changing world. The idea that there is a universally applicable moral law, which is other than the positive law of nations, is not as such a religious idea. But it had its historic roots in the prophetic religion of the Hebrews, with its idea of one creator God, concerned for the welfare of all creation, and especially with those at material and physical disadvantage. Even now a powerful motivation to moral conduct is provided by sincere belief that God wills the flourishing of every human life, and will judge us on our contribution to that divine purpose for the earth. And, in my view, the sense of moral obligation is in itself the impression of the transcendent and supreme goodness of God upon the human mind and heart. Obligation is not, for religious believers, simply a genetically imprinted by-product of ancient struggles for the survival of the human species. It is the impress of a divine reality of pure Goodness upon a human awareness that has been corrupted by selfish desire.

The evils of religion are many, for desire does not exempt religion from its dominion. It so corrupts the heart that it is hard for us to distinguish right from wrong in particular cases. So religion internally reflects the same moral disputes that are raised for all morally serious people, especially by new technological developments in our world. And it reflects the same corruptions of power exercised in the name of morality that disfigure the political life of nations.

But my argument has been that the major world religions have at their heart a concern for personal fulfilment, and place the ideal of such fulfilment in a transcendental or spiritual realm that has primary existence, reality, and value. If that is the case, then the objectivity and categorical moral force of morality can be safeguarded by religious devotion to transcendental Goodness. And religion can reach a fuller rational and moral maturity by placing the quest for personal fulfilment at the centre of its practices and doctrines.

The argument of this book reflects the contemporary interrelation of religion and morality by attempting to show how four great religious traditions have positive and creative vitality that can inspire and reinforce a humanistic or personalistic moral commitment. Yet those religious traditions need fully to embrace the concern for human welfare, for personal flourishing and the flourishing of all sentient life, that the moralists of the Enlightenment showed at their best. At this critical time in the history of the planet earth, religion and morality need to be allies in the quest for human fulfilment and for the fuller flourishing of all life. In isolation religion and morality may atrophy and die. Together they could be an irresistible force for good.